73 Moments in Life

Asterios Balatzis

Copyright © 2023
Asterios Balatzis (Author)
Constantina Constantinou (Illustrator)
All rights reserved.
ISBN: 9798391002888

Introduction

Life is a challenging journey. This book will help you start feeling, thinking, and behaving differently when dealing with life and everyday challenges. Not only will this book help you better deal with others, but this book helps you deal better with yourself.

I have learned 73 moments of key thoughts along my journey. Some ideas are about how we deal with others, and other beliefs are about how we deal with ourselves.

The best way to use these thoughts is to read one daily, reflect on what it communicates, and consider how you feel, think about others and yourself, and how you might change how you deal with others and how you deal with yourself.

Make notes about your reflections and how you intend to change. Try to make those changes in your life and how you deal with everyday challenges. Be true to yourself and your intentions. Use your reflections and notes to fuel your change.

And as you change, let me know how you are doing and if there is anything I can do to support you on your journey.

1

True Colors

If you want to see their true colors, let them be free to do whatever they want.
People tend to show their real character when they feel free.
And knowing who they are from the beginning is best.
This will save you time and feelings.
Why?
Because a person who is scared to show you who they truly are is usually pretending.
And by pretending, they are showing you someone or something else to please you or achieve what they have in mind.
Please don't do it. Don't push them. Let them be free.
Their actions will always speak louder than their words.

73 Moments in Life

2

Search for Your Light

Remember that there is always a light at the end of the road, no matter how hard the days seem or how dark it is around you.
All you must do is keep moving and never give up.
Stay focused on your goals and dreams.
No one will do it for you if you don't chase your goals and dreams.
People usually give up quickly because they focus on their goals instead of their next step.
Remember that even the most minor steps are much more significant than you think.
You will recognize how big those small steps are once you turn your back and see how far you have come from where you began.

73 Moments in Life

3

Control Your Energy

Stay humble and calm.
You don't always have to tell your side of the story.
You know that time will usually express it for you.
Why?
Because people, sooner or later, need to be themselves.
It happens naturally.
Being yourself is not something that anyone can hide for too long.
Time is always your ally, not your enemy.

73 Moments in Life

Don't Rush

Don't rush and get too excited because the grass is greener on the other side.
Remember, sometimes the grass is greener on the other side because it is artificial or fake.
People easily express things that they don't mean in the beginning.
To quickly understand how much they are ready to give, act the way you naturally act in your current situation, and you will see how different they truly are.
Fake can't stay next to real for too long.

73 Moments in Life

5

Fear of the Past

Do not let past fears haunt you.
Don't allow those fears to hold you back with the thought that the present looks like a past experience.
Those thoughts will ruin everything new that comes into your life.
The past will only repeat itself if you have kept what you were doing in the past.
If you really learned your lesson, the past won't repeat itself.

73 Moments in Life

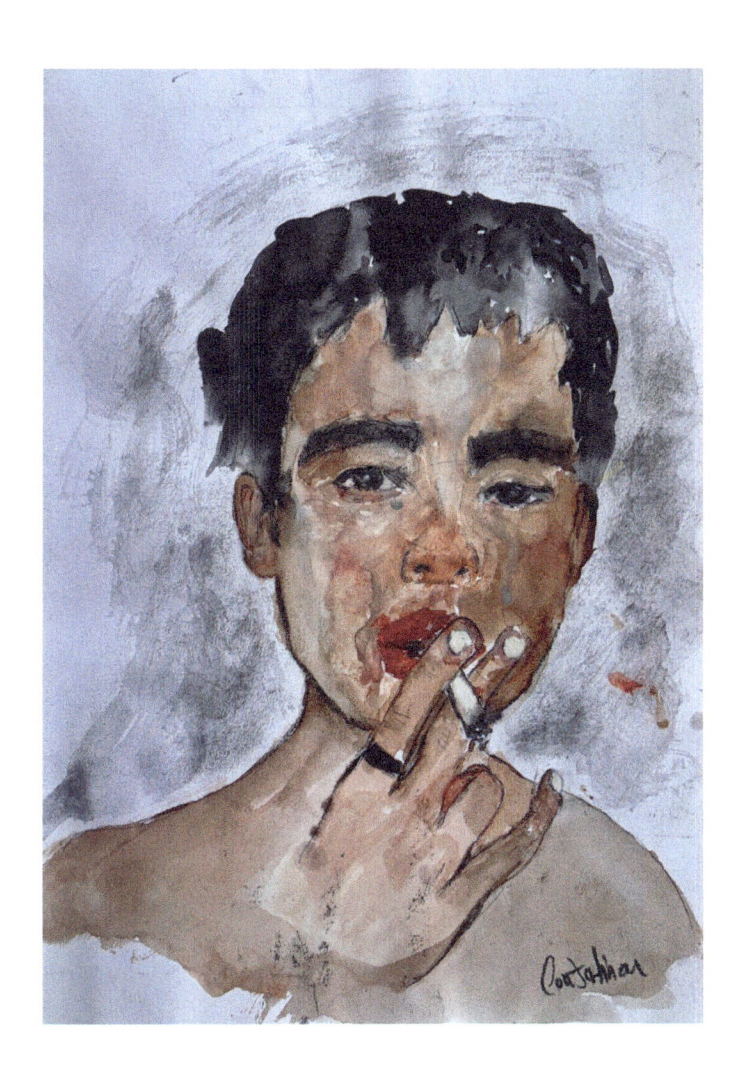

6

A Rhythm for One

Learn not to ask people to dance to the music you're listening to in your head.
If they cannot hear and understand it, but expect you to be able to make them experience it.
Remember, everyone dances to their own music.
Only experienced dancers will know, understand, and be able to dance to your music.

73 Moments in Life

7

When Someone Breaks You

When someone breaks you and leaves you behind, don't wish them pain, but love and healing because what they did, they did out of inner pain caused by a past traumatic experience. People who really love themselves don't hurt anyone. Those who claim to love themselves but really don't are the ones who will seek revenge.

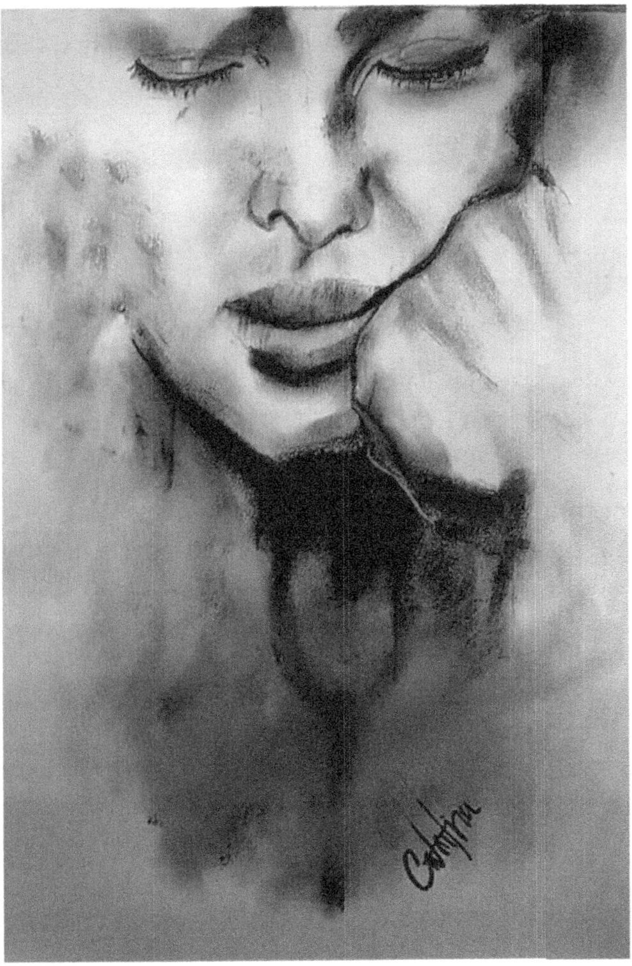

8

To Hold onto Yesterday

Remember that what you felt was inside you.
The feelings, the love, and the appreciation were all yours.
Most of the time, people don't experience what or how you think.
Instead of creating the fantasy that they will feel what you feel, start making your reality of how you will handle the situation if they don't understand what you feel.
So you will be ready and strong to move along your journey.

73 Moments in Life

9

The Courage to be Seen

Never be afraid to show different parts of your character. People will love in some parts, and in others, people will hate. But what matters is those who stayed and tried to understand how they felt, loved, or hated, and instead of judging you, they said, "I'm glad I met you."

73 Moments in Life

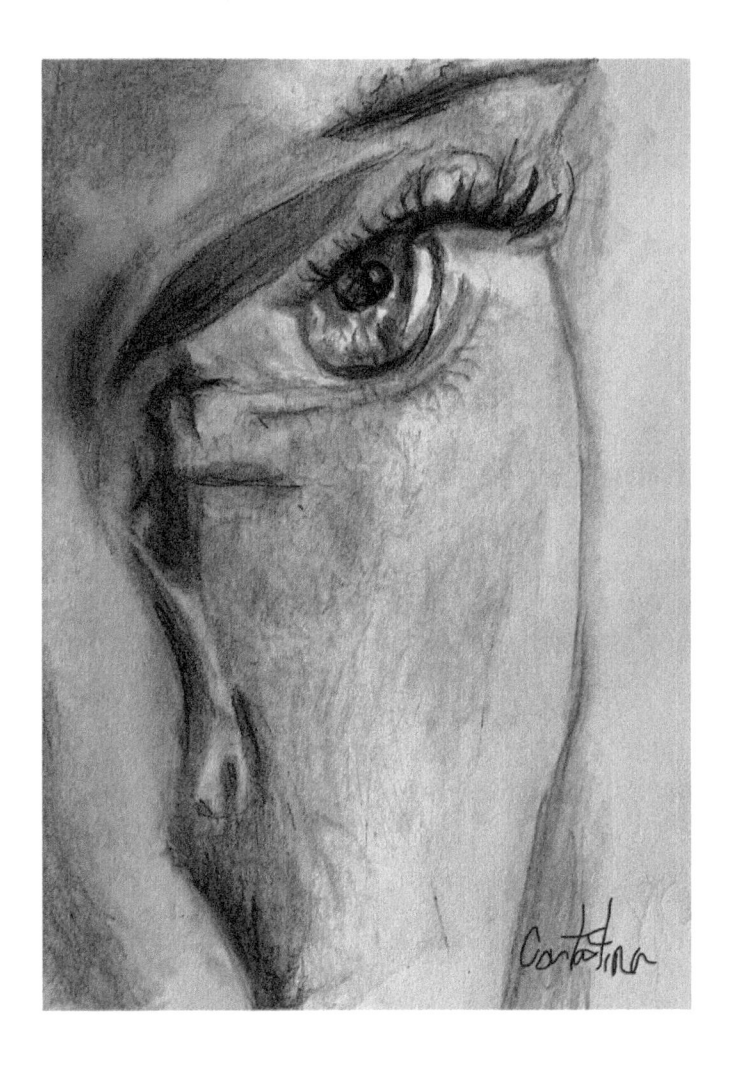

10

One of the Greatest Lessons in My Life

If someone doesn't chase similar dreams as yours, it's time for you to realize that instead of wasting your time in a fantasy, you must bring yourself back to the brutal reality of continuing to chase your dreams and not include those who have stopped dreaming.
Nothing can stop a vision or a dream faster than a person who doesn't have any.

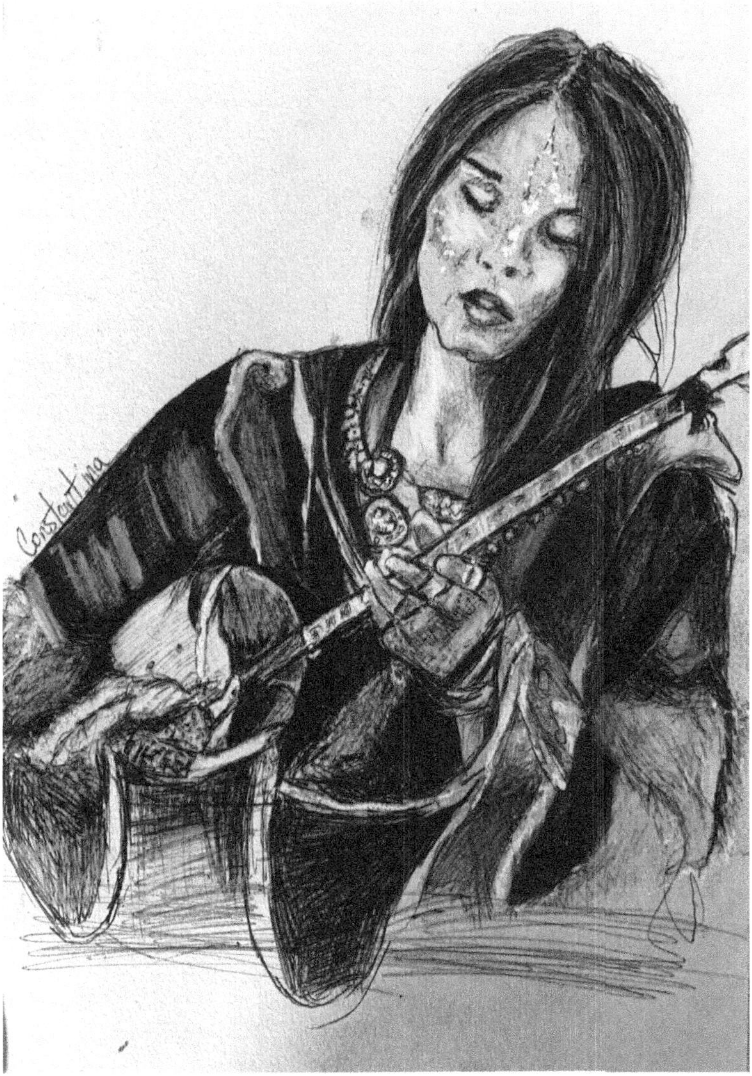
Constantina

11

Keep Your Fire

Believe in yourself.
Keep fueling your fire.
Even if they throw tons of dirty dead water, your fire still burns.
Your ideas, your dreams, your goals, and your passions in life are above everything and everyone.
Never allow anyone to extinguish your fire.
Remember, you have a purpose in this world.
Follow your purpose, even if no one is coming with you.

73 Moments in Life

12

Those Who are Harsh with You are Your Biggest Fans

People who speak harshly with you usually genuinely love and truly believe in you.
The reasons they are so harsh include the following:
First, they fear what you will become and the reality that they will lose the power to influence you.
Second, they are afraid that the rest of the world will see the light you hide in yourself, which scares them more than anything.
Because they know that once everyone sees that light, someone better than them might step into your life.
It's not really hate. Honestly, it's insecurity.

73 Moments in Life

13

A Smile's Simple Gift

Remember to start your day with a smile.
What happened yesterday is history, and you can not change it.
What happens tomorrow is unknown, and it may never be.
So, live today and smile.
Make your day marvelous. Because your mental health matters, this, my friend, is more important than anything.
Remember, the past causes depression, and the future causes anxiety, but you are living today.
Choose your time because you're the only one who is in control.

73 Moments in Life

14

Staying Focused is Never One-Sided

Focusing on your dreams, building your kingdom, and making money is one thing.
The other thing is finding a person who truly loves you.
Because once your greatest supporter is in your home, the negativity, even if it is in your home, will begin to disappear.
Someone will always add wood to fuel your fire and help it burn like never before.
Let's be honest. No King has ever built a great kingdom without his Queen next to him.
History is our most excellent teacher.

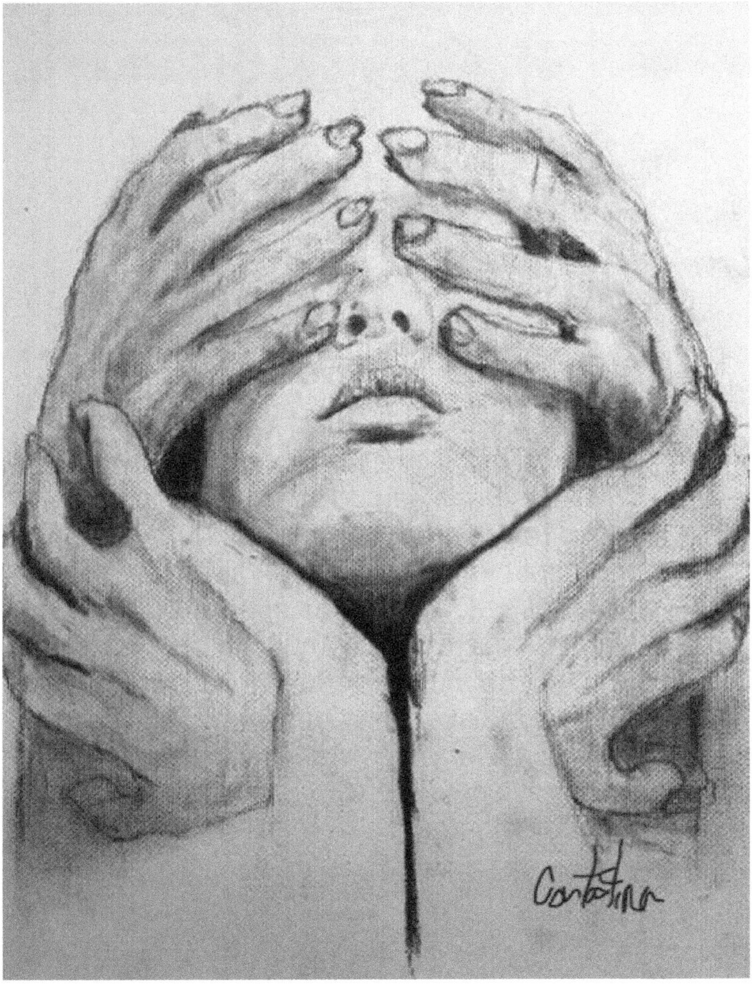

15

Undress Her Soul

Making a woman take off her clothes is the easiest thing to do.
Everyone can do it.
It does not require special skills.
But making a woman trust you enough to undress her soul and show you what is hidden requires special skills.
Trust never comes as a gift but must be earned.
And when people open the hidden parts of their souls to you, they do it because they trust you.
Never betray someone who has shown you their soul.
Otherwise, if you betray someone who has shown you their soul, you can't call yourself a man.

73 Moments in Life

16

Be Careful About What You Share on Social Media

Be careful what you expose on social media about your private life.
There are people out there who live to make other people unhappy.
If they can access your life, they will try to ruin everything with rumors and misinformation and even create "fake facts."
They will do all this because they are unhappy with themselves and hate seeing anyone else be happy around them.

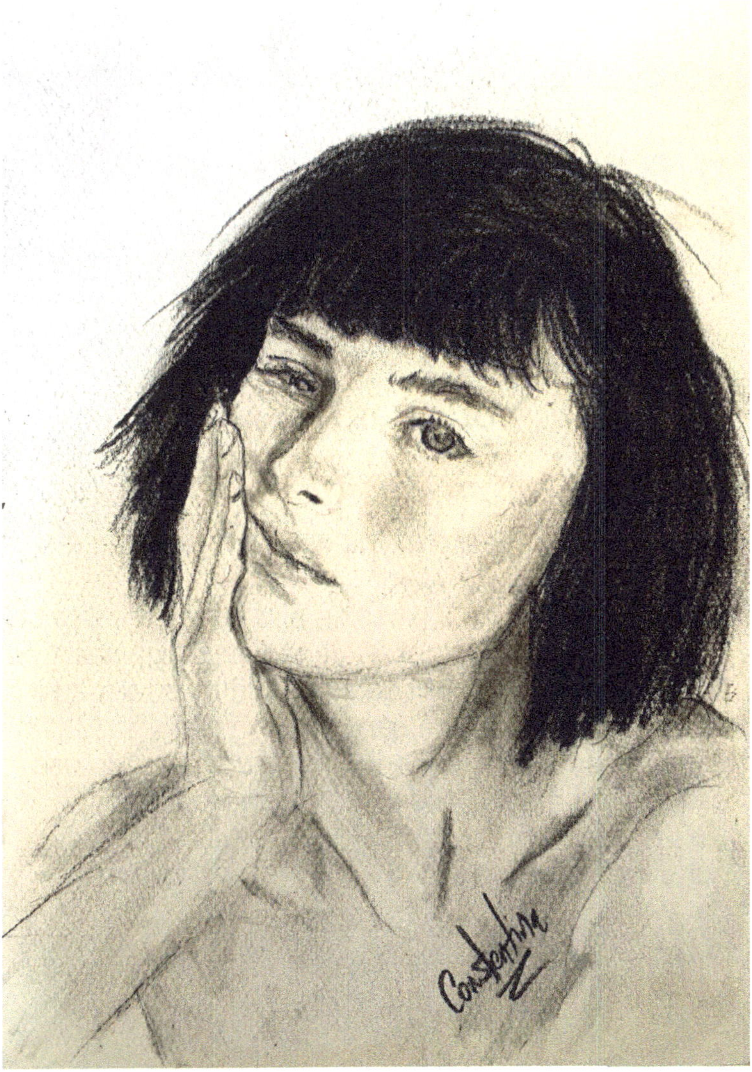
Constantine

17

Your Past

Your past is there for a reason.
Your past contains the lessons you need to learn to move forward.
Learn to use your past as a blessing and not as a curse.
Because once you realize that the experience you gained from your past is essential, you will be surprised by how many beautiful things you can create in life.
Everything happens for a reason, and it's up to you to use these blessings to create a positive or negative present and future.
Use your experience wisely.

73 Moments in Life

18

Sometimes, You Move Forward

Many times in life, you seemingly move forward.
You gain new things, new people, new experiences, new memories, and much more.
But your soul is always in a different place and cannot let go.
Why is this happening?
There are two reasons:
First, the regret of not trying something and never knowing the outcome.
Second, your childhood ego is still in touch with those memories.
Some will say this is because you found your soulmate there.
But if that were the case, you must remember one undisputed rule:
Those who genuinely love a person never move on.
So, if you both have moved on, you were not soulmates, and all that exists now is the regret of not knowing the results of that particular situation.

73 Moments in Life

19

Silence is Your Friend

Silence is your friend during times of isolation.
During such times, you can receive answers you missed
hearing and understanding during your noisiest times.
Learn to appreciate silence.
You'll understand that silence is always your best friend when
you do.

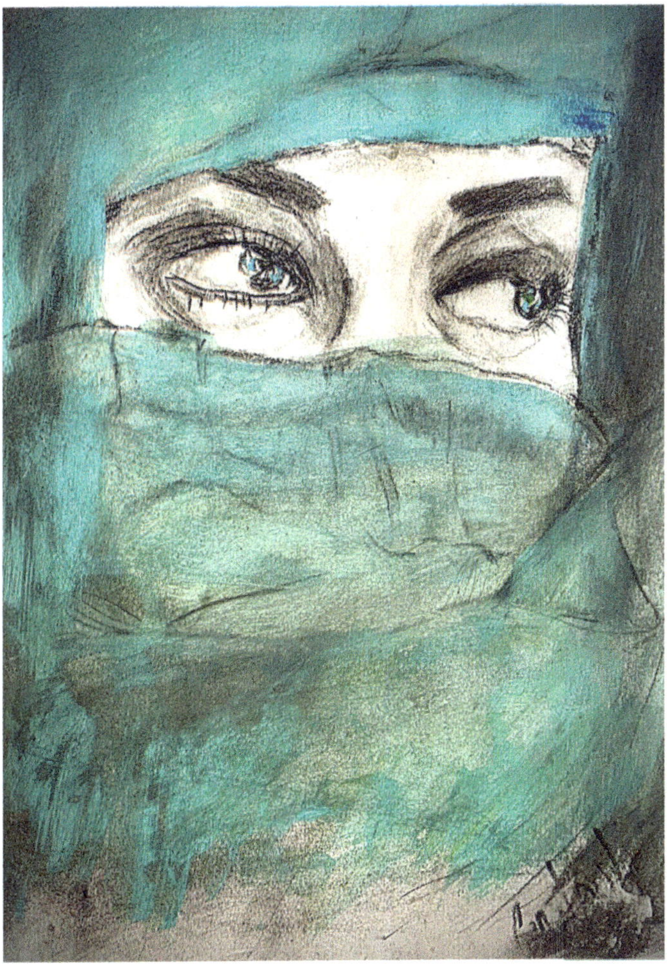

20

The Cost of Wasted Time

Refrain from wasting your time thinking that something will change.
Nothing will change if you don't decide to act toward your own happiness.
Always remember, people change not because they are told to change but because they want to.
So, it's up to you.
Keep going in circles and blaming everyone for wrong decisions or fix yourself and make the right decisions.

73 Moments in Life

21

You Can't Move On Without Them

The main reason you can't move on without them is that something is holding you back.
And what is holding you back is often not even real.
Sometimes, you think they are thinking about you; sometimes, they do.
But thinking that they are calling you back is really just in your own thoughts, your own ambitions, your own expectations, and your own wishes.
Remember, when they left you, they made a decision that comforts themselves and, above all, a new starting point that doesn't include you.
So, do yourself a favor and start living again.
What is to come, will come, and what is to go, will go.

73 Moments in Life

How Your Parents Raised You is Important

How we are raised by our parents is very important.
This is the basis for living life, processing information, and dealing with our problems throughout life.
But what we become beyond this foundation is based on our inner work, which we do ourselves.
The life we live, we create on our own.
So, having a healthy foundation is really important, but building a healthy life beyond our foundation is much more essential.
Remember, your parents and no one else lives in your head twenty-four-seven.
You live in your head, and it's up to you to live in paradise or hell.

73 Moments in Life

23

When You are Overthinking

When you're starting to overthink, stop yourself for a second and ask yourself:
Is what I'm thinking real?
Does what I'm feeling really exist?
Or are these just fake scenarios that my thoughts have started creating?
Because most of the time, what makes us overthink is the unknown.
So, be an adult, ask questions, and seek answers.
And if they lie to you, don't worry. Lies stay hidden for a short time.
The first thing that reveals lies are reactions to your questions.
If they hide something, you will get the vibe on the spot.
Trust your gut and make the decision to stay or leave.
But no matter what, stop hurting yourself for something that probably isn't real.

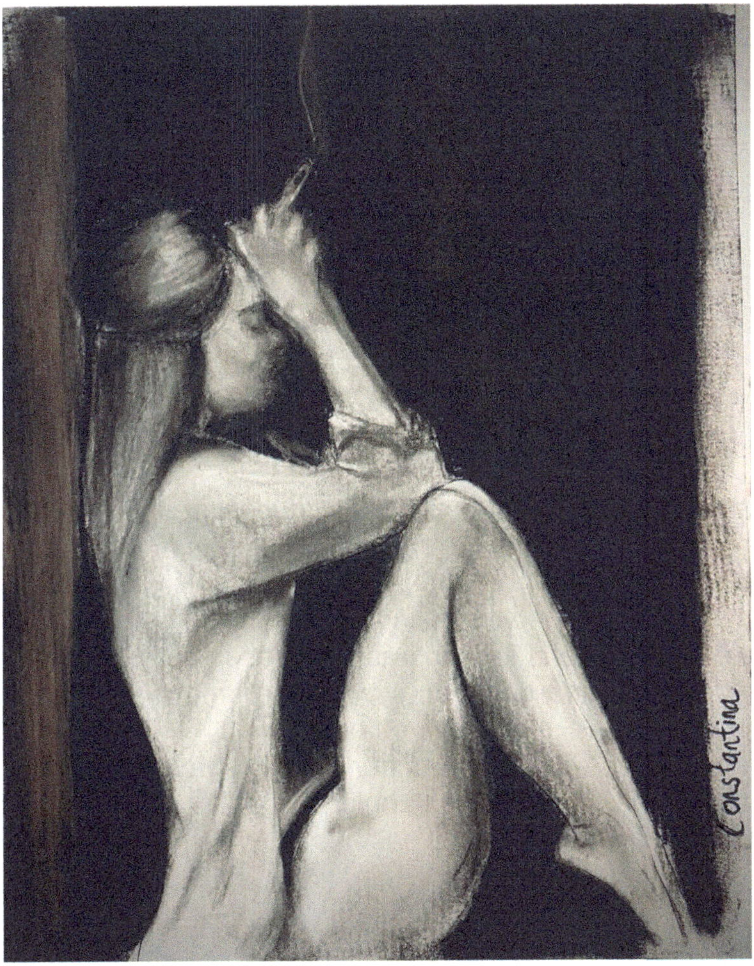
Constantina

24

The Journey Forward

Never allow anyone from your past to come and ruin your future.
Your past will always come back when your future looks bright and perfect.
It's the test you receive from the universe to see if you learned your lesson.
Whatever happens in your past, let it be in the past.
After all, if it was meant for you, it will never return after you have moved on.
And even if it does return, remember that you have moved on and are happier.
Smile, and never go back to the past.

73 Moments in Life

25

Love has No Borders

When you genuinely love, nothing can hold you back.
No distance, no work, no age difference, nothing.
You will move mountains just to be where you want to be.
You won't find excuses but find reasons to make it happen.
Most of the time, to determine if what you are feeling is real love or just enthusiasm, all you need is three months, and you will be able to see if it is real love or just something you want.
After three months, if this feeling remains, then believe me, you will do everything possible to be where you want to be.

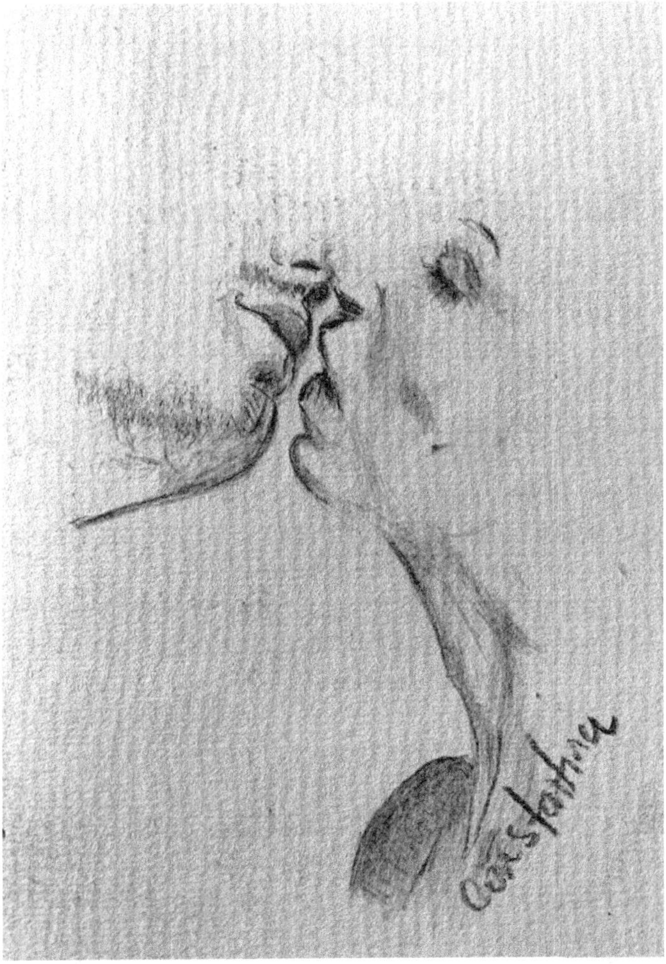

26

When a Man Doesn't Feel Appreciated, He Stops

When a man stops feeling appreciated, he stops trying.
A man always wants to make his woman happy by being romantic, giving her flowers, taking her to restaurants, and being friendly.
A man stops when he does things in public; instead of receiving a positive reaction from his woman, he gets a negative response.
For example, a man hears, "Don't you ever embarrass me like that," or "You know how I feel out in the world when you act like a teenager."
Or when he cleans the house to hear, "You didn't put those things in order" or "You did it wrong."
At this point, a man stops.
And men stop it because they realize they get the opposite instead of receiving positive vibes.
So ladies, remember, men never try to do things when they don't receive the validation that what they are doing pleases them.

73 Moments in Life

27

None of Those Defines Who You Are

Your age doesn't define your maturity, your grades don't limit your intelligence, and rumors don't determine who you are.
So, let people talk. They always do.
Just make sure to take small steps to better yourself every day.
After all, what matters the most is how you see yourself in the mirror every day and not how others see you.
Those who genuinely want to see who you are will explore you and see what everyone else can't see.

73 Moments in Life

28

Respect People

Respect people, and understand them.
Why are they who they are?
Why do they act the way they do?
Remember, none of us sit high enough to look down on other people.
Always remember, everyone walks their own path with different experiences.
The place they are today and all their struggles may become your home tomorrow.?

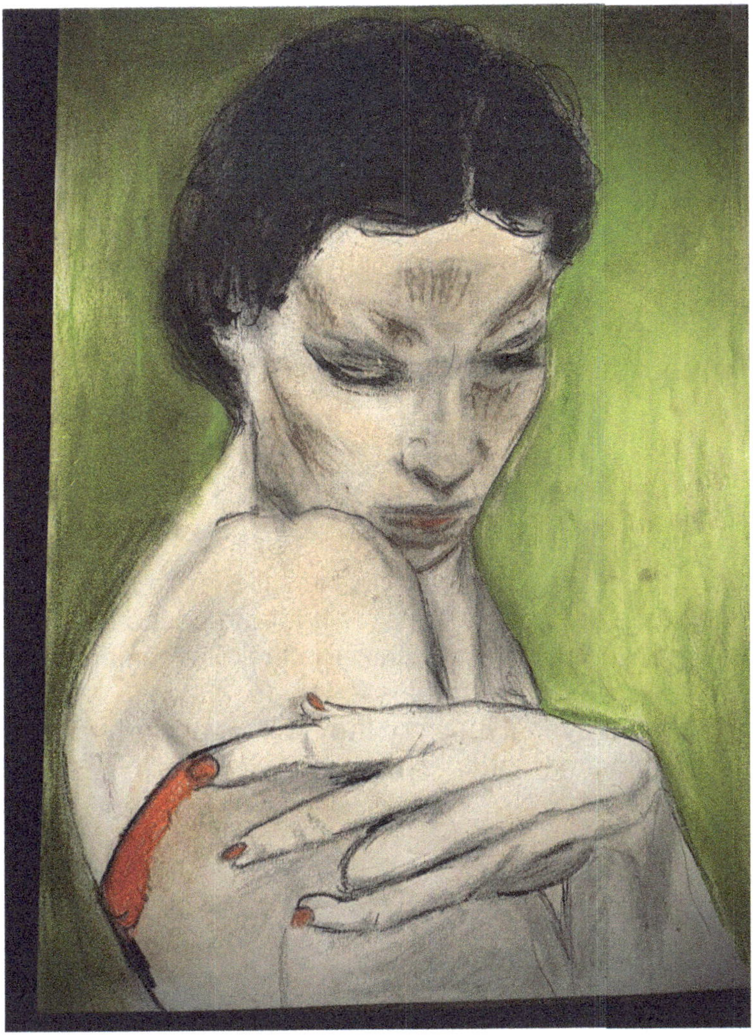

29

Bring Peace into People's Lives

Remember, when you get into someone's life, even if you find them in one piece or in many parts, bring them peace because most of those who had passed through their life couldn't do what you are blessed to do.
Use that blessing; even if they go, they will always remember you as something extraordinary.

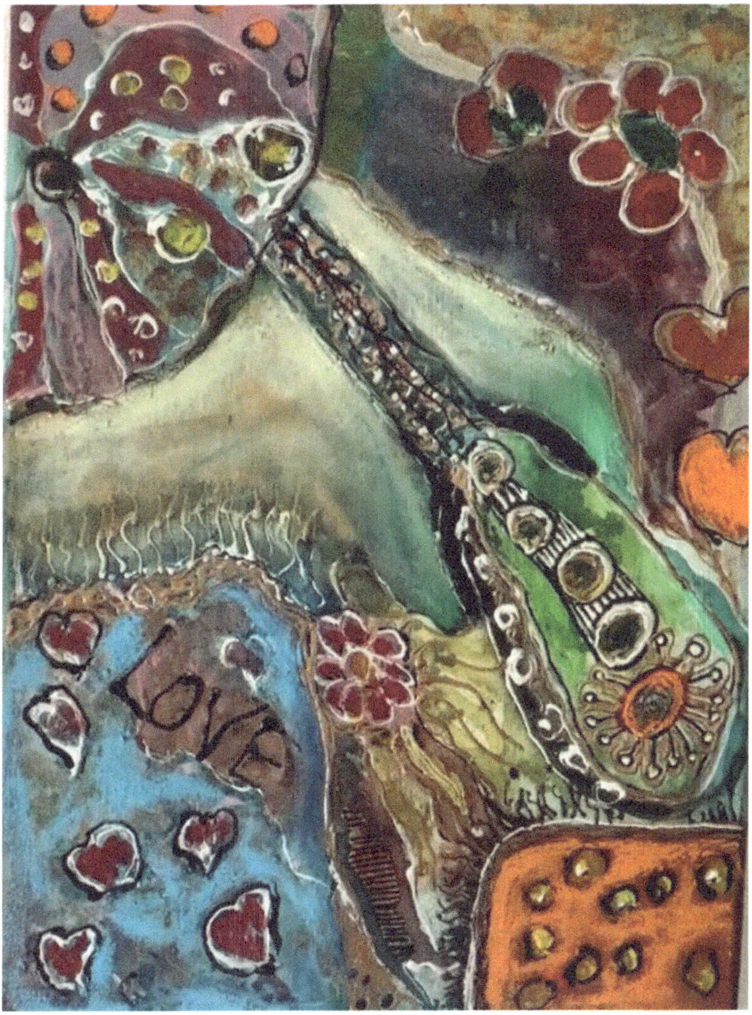
LOVE

30

They Will Live in Your Dreams Forever

Even if you don't want to admit it, they will live in your dreams forever.
Why?
Because with this particular person, you had a soul connection, which is why you can't forget them.
You see, touching the soul of someone is something unique, and just like you can touch someone's soul, the same energy comes and connects you too.

73 Moments in Life

31

When You Can't Put Them in a Better Situation

If you can't put them in a better situation than where they are now, don't speak about their situation.
And what do I mean?
Talking about someone's current situation without the will or power to change is like declaring to the world that you are full of words and no actions.
You may believe that the world will stay focused on your words and miss seeing your actions, but in the end, everything will reflect negatively on you.
So, learn to open your mouth and speak about someone else's life only when you can add something and make it better, Otherwise, stay silent forever.

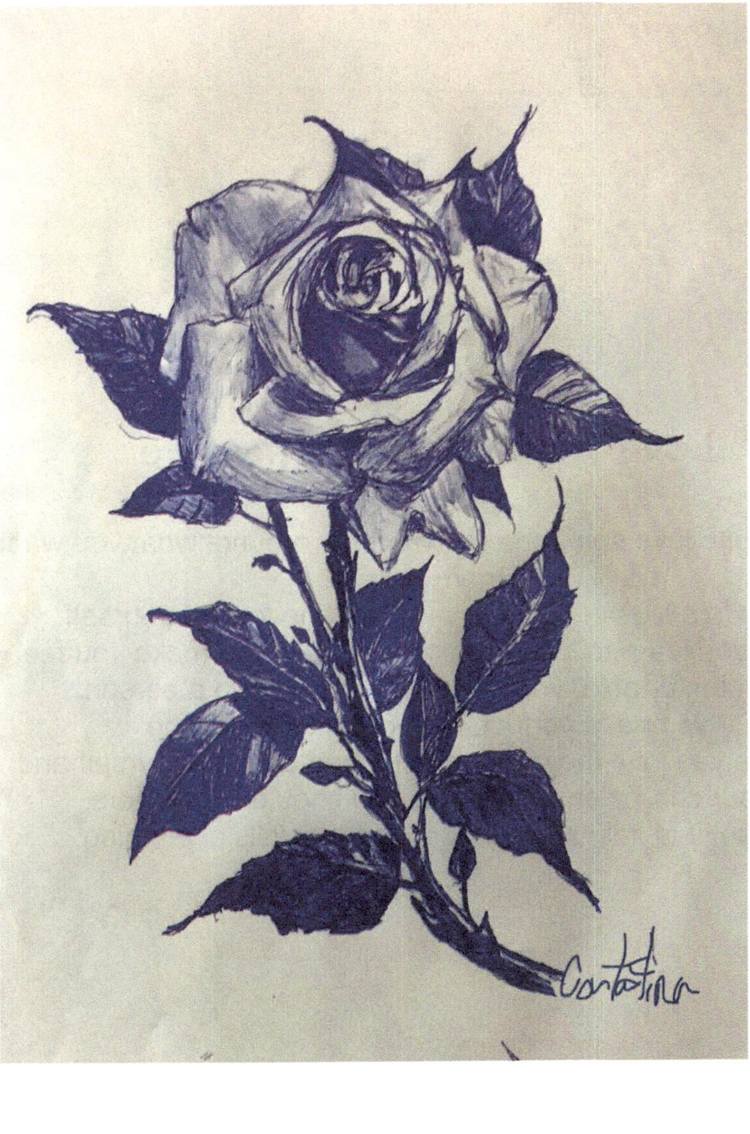

32

Love Them for Who They Are

Learning to love someone for who they are, not what you want them to be.
This is a sign of maturity and genuine love of yourself.
When you learn to love the parts of them that make you feel uncomfortable, you genuinely start loving a person.
No one is perfect, not you, me, or anyone.
So, like you love the good and the bad parts of yourself and your character, this is how you should love others.
Otherwise, it is not love. It is just ego that kills everything.

73 Moments in Life

33

Learn to Forgive

If they don't want to be with you, let them go.
If they ever decide to come back, accept them.
The glory you hide in your soul is something bigger than them.
Remember that everyone can change if they truly want to change.
We all deserve a second chance to fix things like you, me, and everyone.
They deserve the same opportunity.
Sometimes people realize that the decisions they made were wrong.
Sometimes it takes months, even years.
Everyone learns their lessons in life at a different pace.
So, if you have learned your lessons, keep people out because it took them longer to learn their lessons.
What is most important is showing that you are growing.
Let's admit it, they were the ones you loved the most.

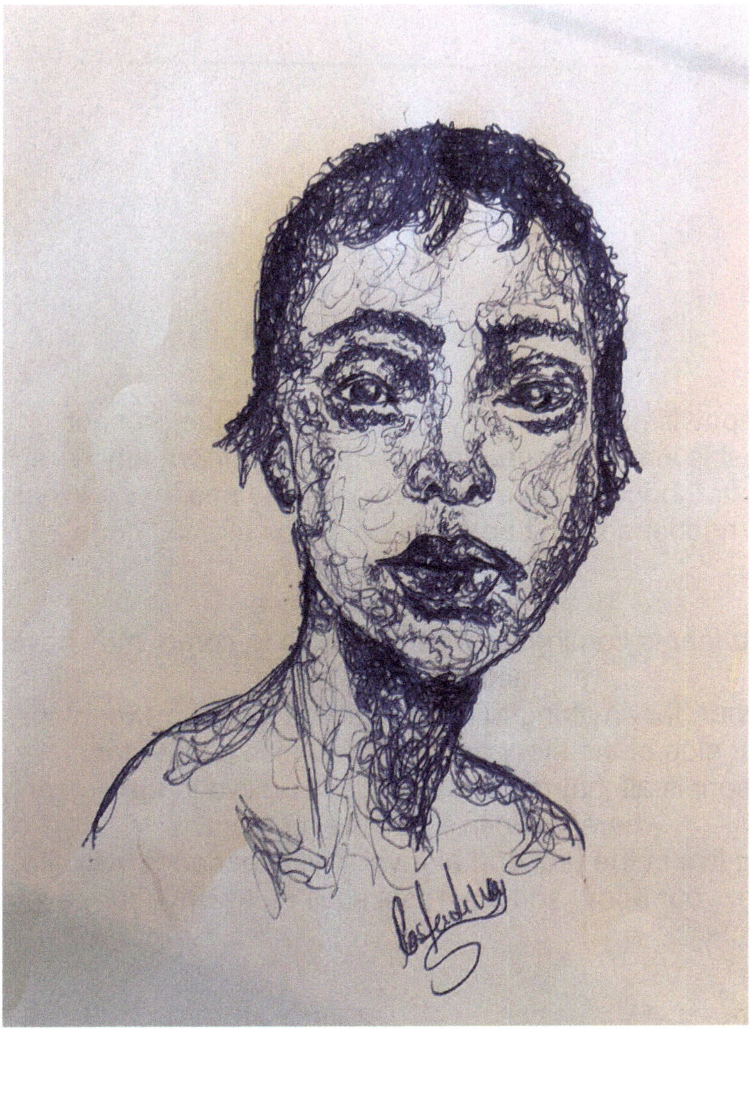

34

Tip for a Better Life

A happy life starts when you start living in the present.
The past is already gone, and you don't live there anymore.
Only your thoughts and memories bring the past back. What has happened can't be changed and is already done.
How about the future?
The future has yet to arrive.
What you fear is coming, or what you wish to come, may never actually arrive.
Remember, for anything to happen, there must be two things, your side of the story and the other side of the story.
The present is all that matters because you live in the present, where you can enjoy the moment.
Learn to live in the present, and you will experience your life, your face, your body, and your soul smiling, twenty-four-seven.

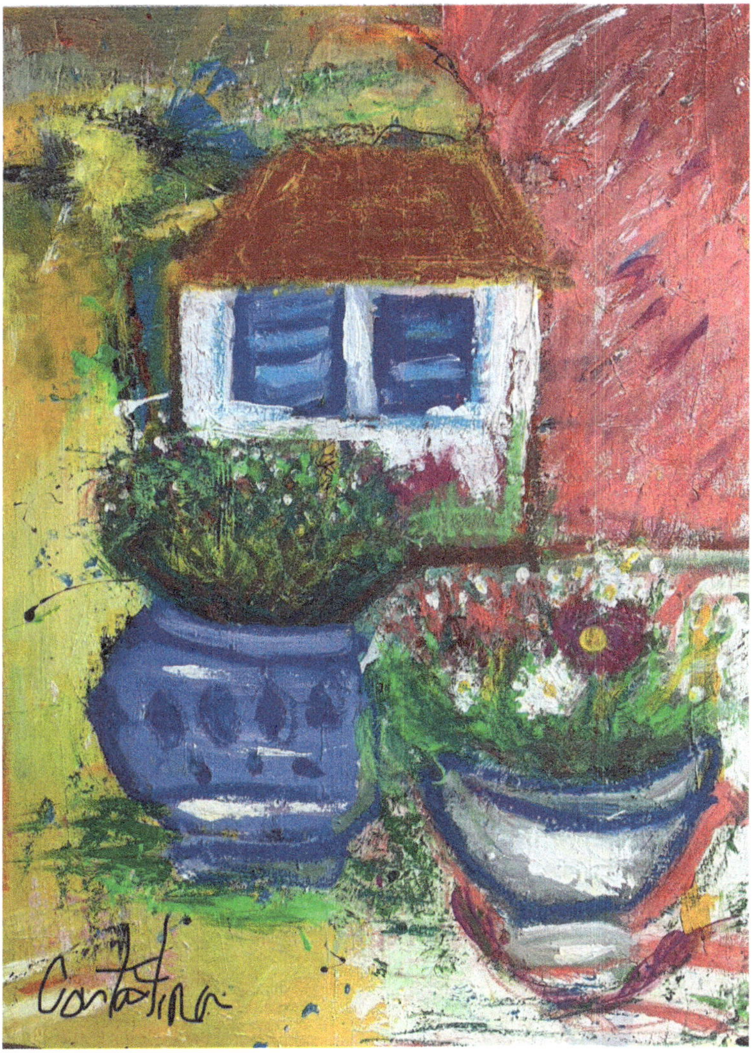
Contatina

35

Being Authentic is Really Hard

Being authentic is very hard because it demands so much energy many need.
People are more comfortable pretending than showing their authentic selves because they know that if they show their true character, many won't like them, so they pretend.
You, me, and many others forget that pretending only attracts the wrong people because when we act, we are not ourselves and aren't real.
Learn to be yourself.
Never be afraid to show parts of your character.
If people go, they aren't your people.
The ones who stay are those who really matter.
Those who see and decide to love and appreciate your perfections and your imperfections are the ones who matter.
And in the end, that's all that matters.

73 Moments in Life

36

Three Ways You Make the Worst Decisions in Your Life

First way: go out to shop or make a deal while hungry.
When you are hungry for food or success, you usually make fast decisions that you often later regret.
Second way: call, text, or start an argument when you are drunk.
You can't think straight at that moment, and even if you may achieve what seems like a positive result, most of the time, it will lead you to your worst decisions.
And finally, but most importantly, never choose your partner when you are horny or lonely.
Why?
Once you put someone in your life because you need them, you immediately turn yourself from a priority to an option because the fear of losing them is greater than the wellness of choosing them.

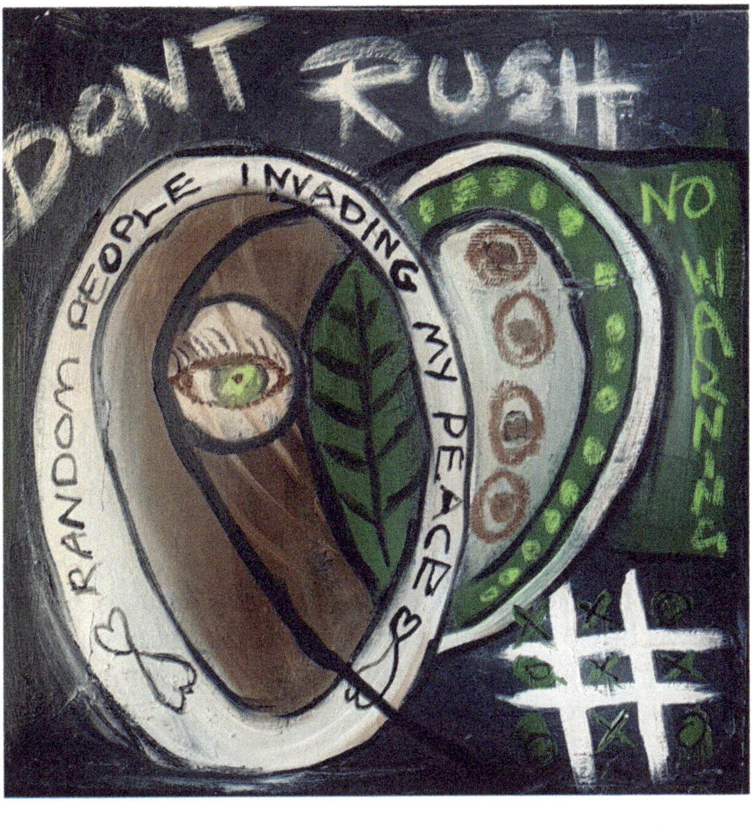
DON'T RUSH
RANDOM PEOPLE INVADING MY PEACE
NO WARNINGS

37

Life Lesson

Instead of focusing on your goals, which may seem far away and challenging, change your mindset and focus on every small step towards your goals.
When you start doing that, you immediately get motivated to move faster and try harder.
And when you look back, you will realize just how far you have advanced from the beginning, and once this sinks in, believe me, you will be so motivated that nothing can stop you.
You will think more intelligently, act wiser, and become more successful than ever imagined.

73 Moments in Life

38

The Courage to Persist

Learn to never give up in life.
Stay consistent in what you're doing.
Sometimes, it takes days. Sometimes, it takes weeks. And sometimes, it takes years.
But, as long as you don't give up and stay focused on what you are doing, you will be successful sooner or later.
Never forget that the biggest lie the world told you is that this is not for you.
Prove the world wrong.

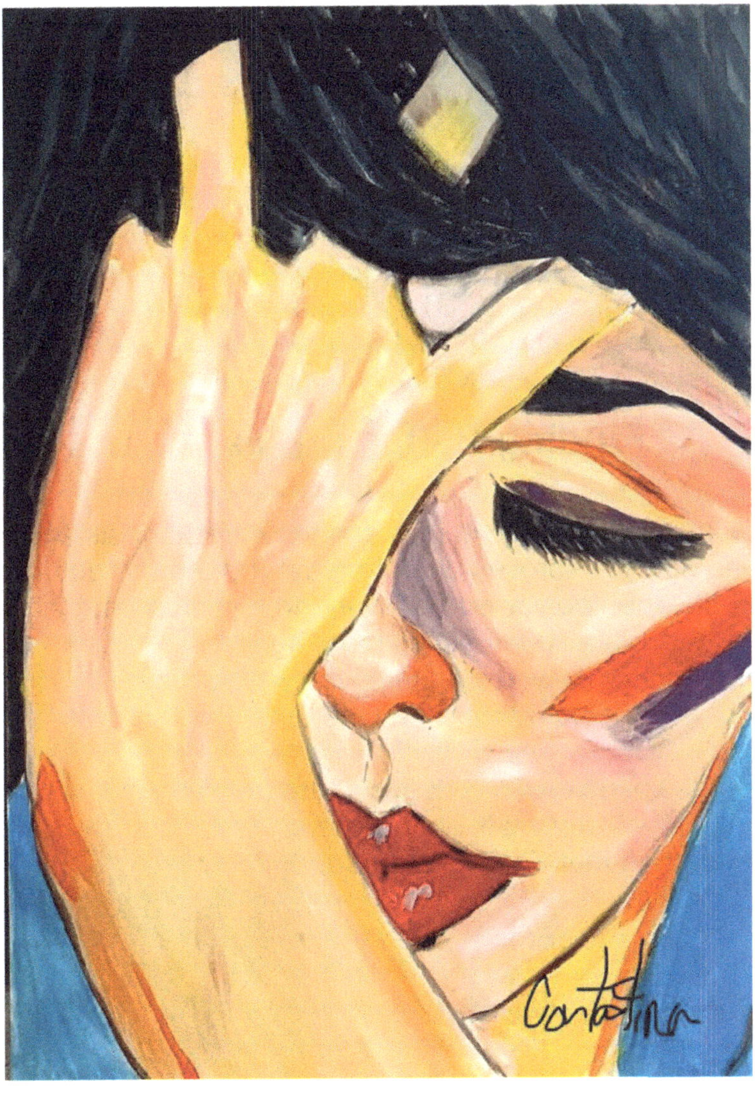

39

Finding Better Tables

If, at the table where you sit, they don't talk about goals and ideas and how to improve your future but instead talk about other people, then do yourself a favor and stand up from that table and never sit there again.
Believe it or not, once you stand up, you will be the next topic being discussed at the table.
Why?
Because those people who lack goals, dreams, and motivation only talk about others.
You're better than that. Get out of there.

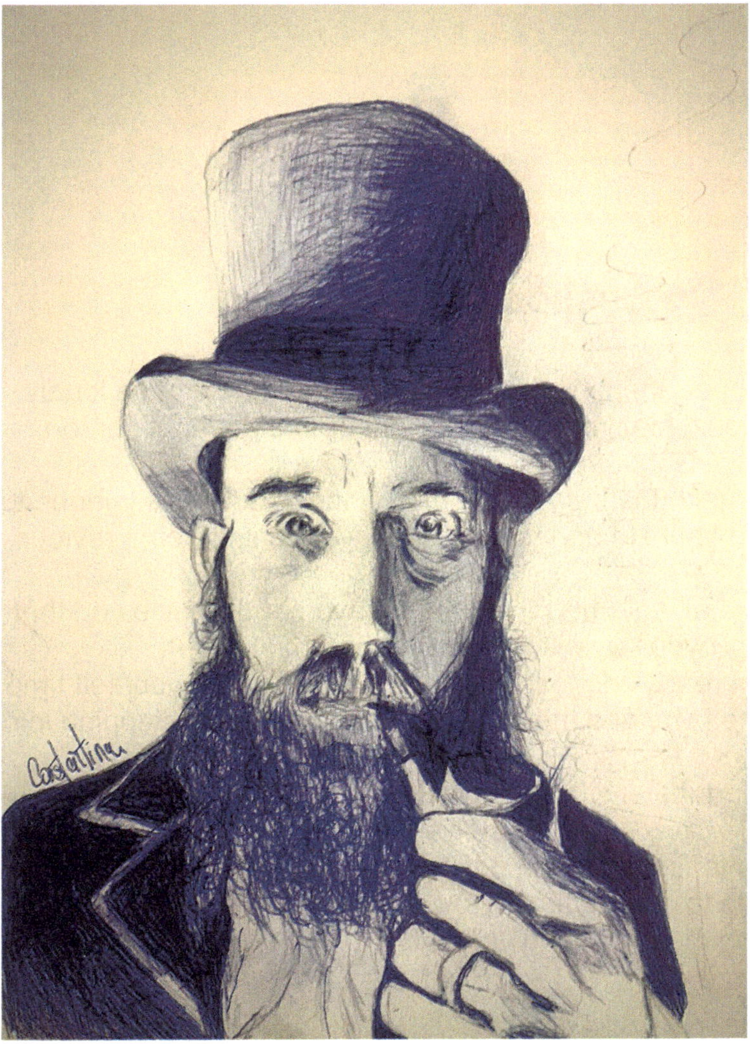

40

Lesson to be Learned

The proper attention from the wrong person during a lonely time could fool you into thinking they are the right person.
Why?
You will make the biggest mistake when you allow someone to step into your life and you have not yet healed from previous trauma.
So, like that, you miss things and have needs inside you that you haven't discovered and healed yet.
So, you are making fast decisions without giving yourself time to see the facts and the colors of the new person stepping into your life.
Unfortunately, this usually leads to one of your worst decisions.
Learn to first heal and fulfill yourself, and only then allow someone to enter your life and add to your happiness versus thinking they will bring you joy.

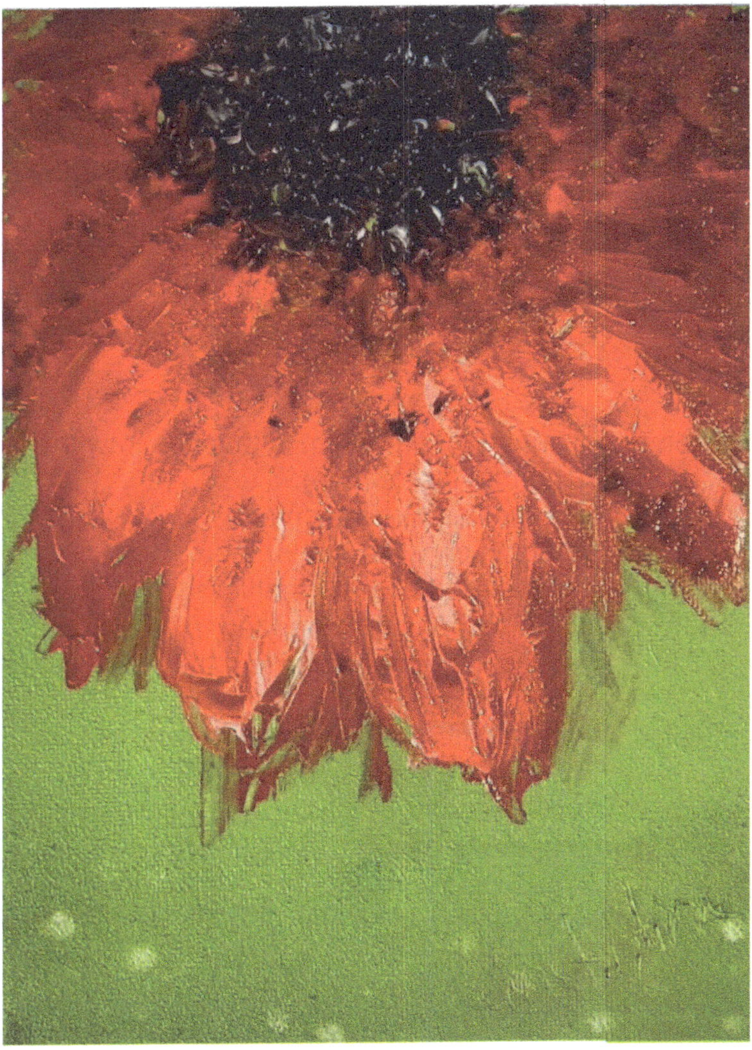

41

You Were Different

The difference between you and them is that you saw the human inside them.
What is the mistake they made?
They thought you were one of them.
Don't blame them, they needed to learn that lesson, and if they had already learned it, perhaps they needed to return to it.
They would keep walking in the same circle if they had yet to learn it.
You, yes you, make sure that you keep moving on.
If they catch up with you, fine.
If they don't catch up with you, accept that they were just another person who came to gain this lesson, use it, or keep doing the same.
Time will show the reality.

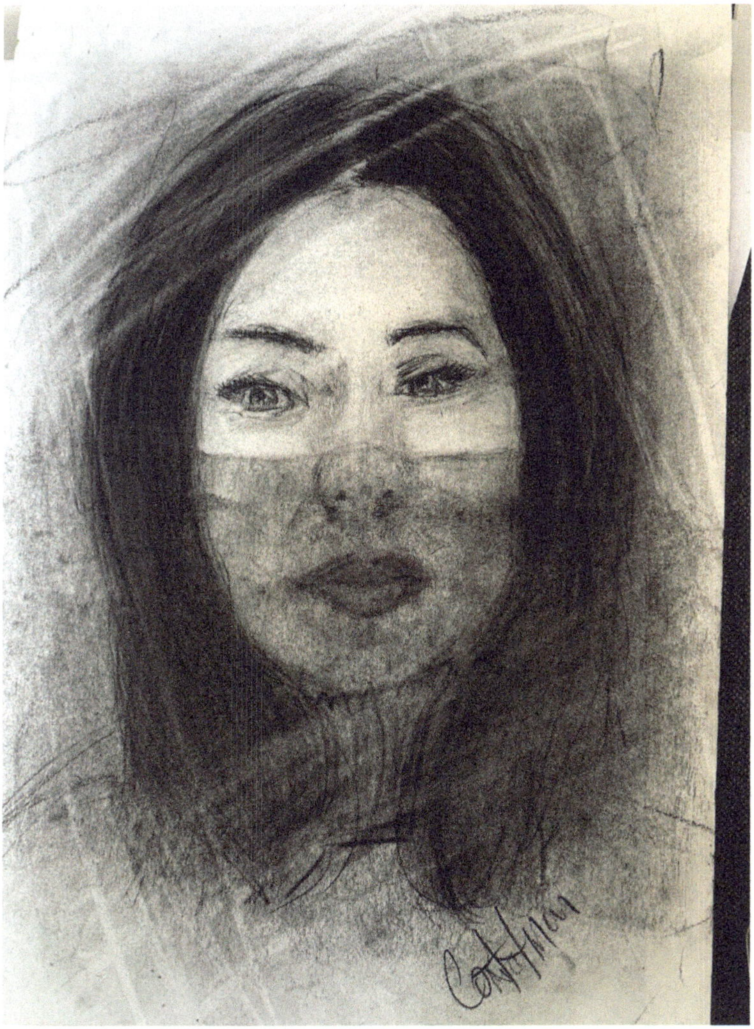

42

Learn This

When you don't ask, the answer will always be a NO.
When you stop trying, the results will always be a FAILURE.
When you go after what you want, it may still be something you will never get.
And when you don't step forward, you will always be in the same place.
So, stop being afraid to ask, change, try, or move.
Even if you lose most of the time, the satisfaction of one win is more significant than all the previous losses.

I LOVE
BLACK
Boom
No
or BLUE
SOMETIMES Green
I Don't Like PINK
Constant

43

Tip for a Good Life

Learn to carefully choose the company you spend time with and share your thoughts and ideas.
Because the company that surrounds you is usually the reason you are being lifted up or put down.
Avoid negativity and add positivity.
Remember, even if you are positive, if you surround yourself with negative people, you will be negatively impacted in trying to reach your goals.
What do negative people do?
Because negative people are incapable of going higher, they try to hold others down at rock bottom with them, so they don't feel lonely.

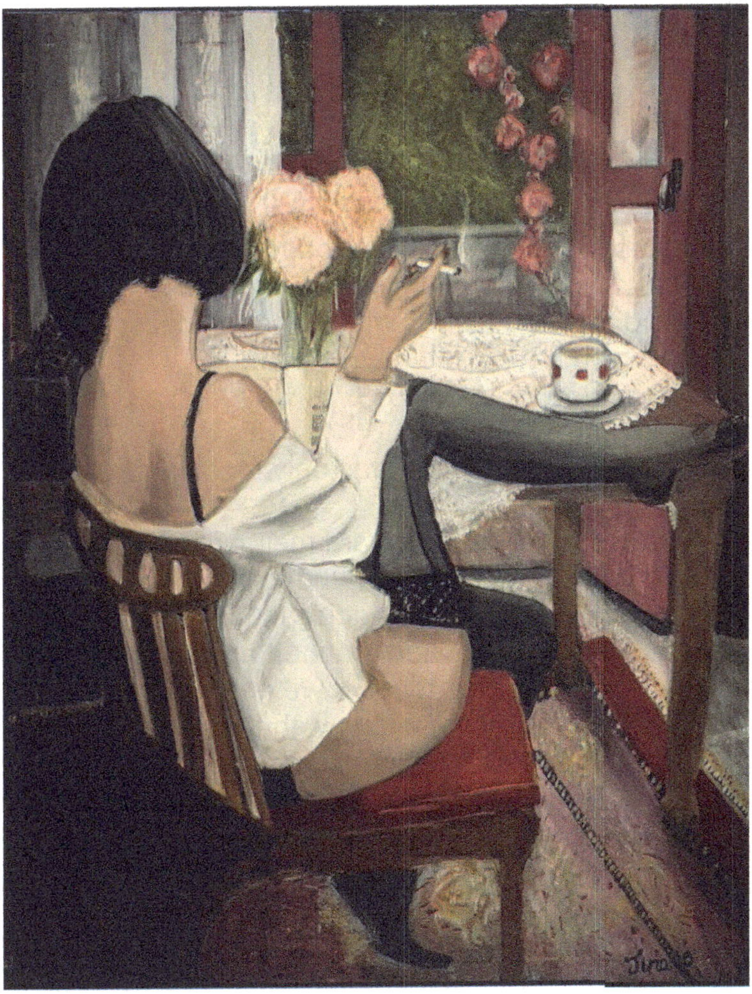

The Hardest Thing to Realize

Make sure to distinguish the history you have with someone, your future plans, and the changes that are about to come.
Just because you have a history with someone doesn't mean you have a future with them.
Sometimes, some travel next to us until we reach a particular spot.
Their contribution to our journey was only reaching that spot with us.
Now, they have to move on toward their own paradise.
And deciding to move out of our life, and for us to move out of their life, is the most significant sign.
Because our shared journey had reached an endpoint, they may have reached their top, but we must change.
There is nothing wrong with that.
At this moment, what attaches you to them are the memories and the daily habits you had created with them, but even if you can't see it now, you will see it in the future.
Understand that dreams, goals, and plans might look similar at some point, but ambitions might change.
So, if you or they have different ambitions, it is better to accept that your and their shared journey was only meant to reach a specific point.
The faster you realize this, the better the results.

73 Moments in Life

45

Lesson to be Learned

The hard truth must be accepted: you can't force someone to love you.
It is up to them.
Love is a personal feeling.
And here comes the more brutal truth.
You have to realize that you must stop trying to love someone who doesn't want to love you.
This is a decision that is necessary for your mental health.
Why?
Because even if you know the truth, hope keeps you focused on them, hoping that something might change, but let me remind you that things don't change with your presence but with your absence.
People change when you are not around anymore and when they realize if they are better with or without you.

73 Moments in Life

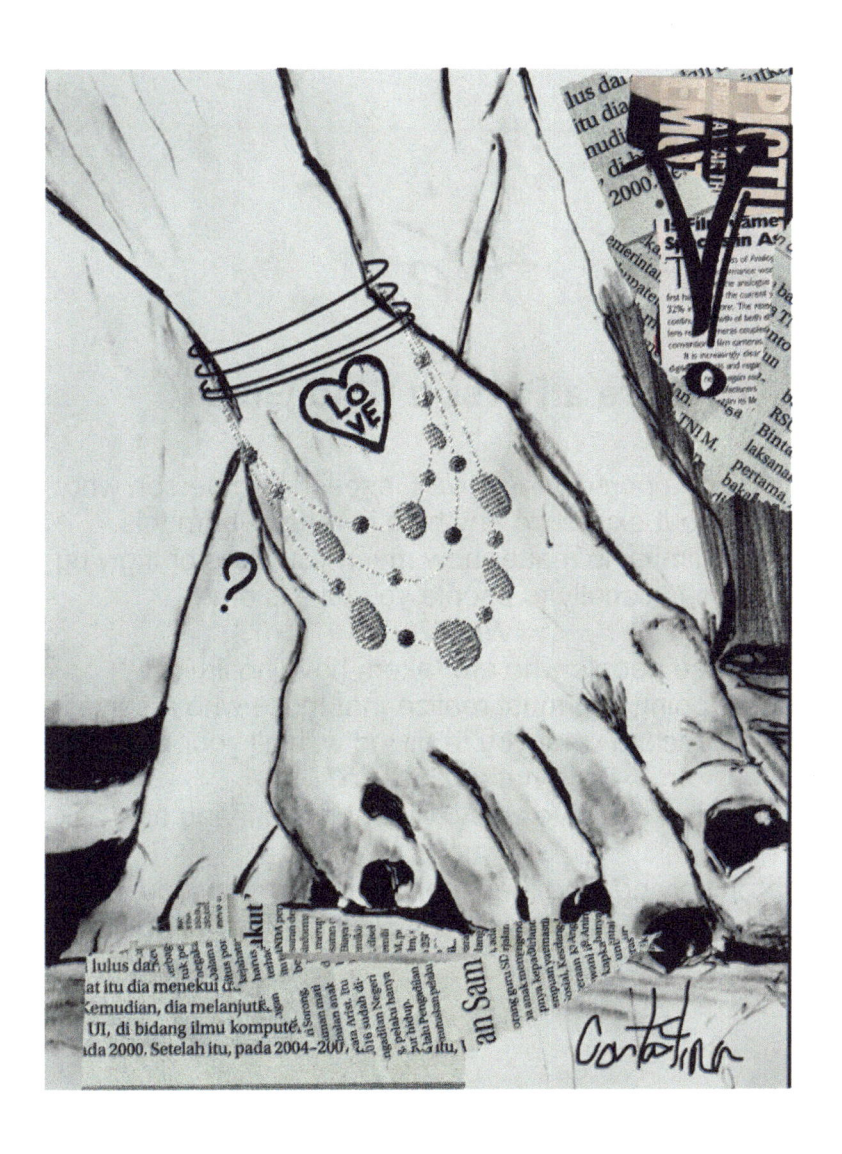

46

If You're a Person Who Gives

When you are a person who gives, especially a person who gives without expecting anything in return, learn this.
You must set limits no matter how much you have or if giving unconditionally to people you love is okay.
Why?
Because people who are takers have no limits.
And at some point, you must realize that those who receive it do not appreciate what you're giving with all your heart.
So, what do they do?
They throw what you give away without using it and only ask for more.
So, you aren't giving, and they aren't receiving, but you're just wasting the best of yourself for people who don't appreciate you and are just taking.

73 Moments in Life

93

47

A Moment to Treasure

Remember that it is necessary to change the current version of yourself who keeps bringing the same types of people into your life.
Most of the time, we lack seeing this issue that we carry inside us, and we think that everyone is the same, but in the end, the changes we haven't made in ourselves keep bringing the same types of people into our lives.
So, always remember to remind yourself that you are here for a reason, and this reason is not for any of those people.
You have to figure out what you are doing, and once you do, you will be more positive, and everything will change in your life.
Remember that we don't become what we dream of but what we think and do.

73 Moments in Life

48

One of the Hardest Pills

One of the hardest pills you will ever swallow is that you will be judged by people who don't even know your story.
Unfortunately, many people judge.
Many people judge because instead of using their vision, they use past experiences and compare you with something or someone historically in their life.
You can't do anything about it.
Most of the time, this happens because they miss something inside them.
Often, what they miss is accepting the fact that most people are similar but different.
So, if you ever meet a person who is quick to judge you based on their past traumatic experiences, move on.
They still have a lot of work to do, and it's not your job to fix them. It's their job to better themselves.

73 Moments in Life

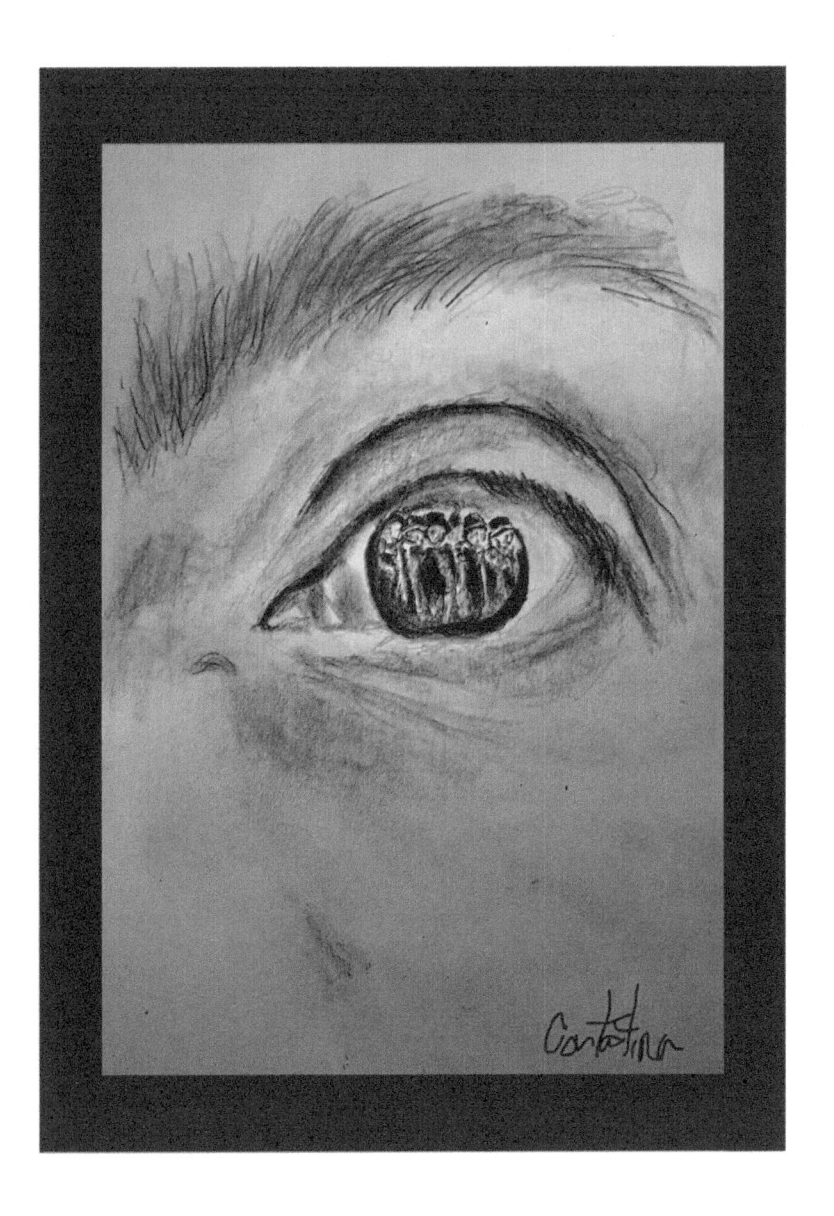

49

Always Remember

A person who cries easily has a lot of pain and a good heart.
A person who gets angry quickly is a person who is tired of fighting alone.
And a person who seems challenged had fought everything alone and was forced to lift themselves up all alone because everyone who said they loved them got lost when they were needed most.

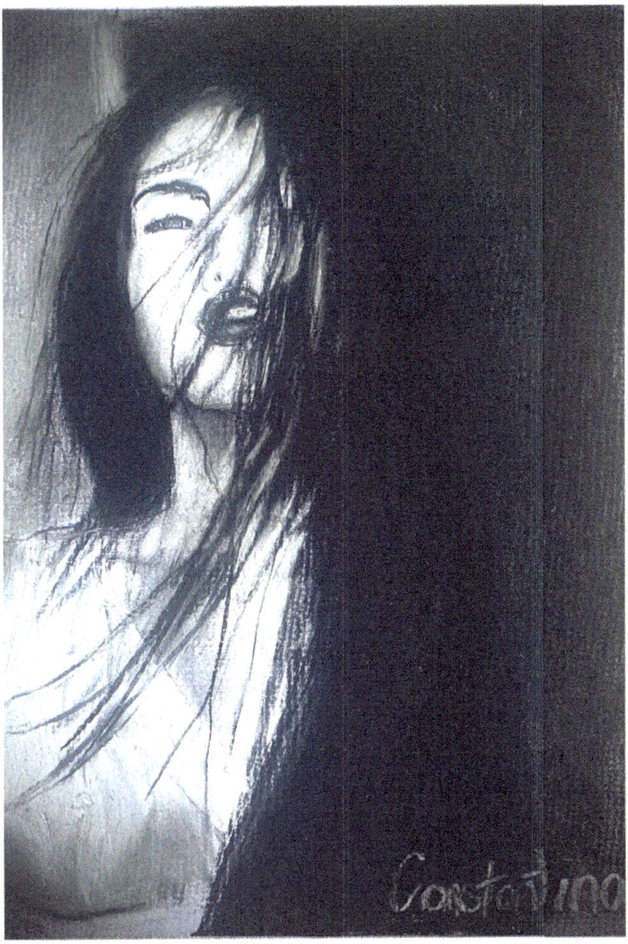
Constantina

50

Everything Happens for a Reason

Remember that in life, everything happens for a reason.
Sometimes it hurts and sends us into depression, where we realize and fix our mistakes.
Initially, it is challenging because we cannot fight our feelings. But, in the end, everything happens. It happens so you can become a better person.
Learn those lessons and become your best version so the world can see and say, "Damn, I want to be like him or her."

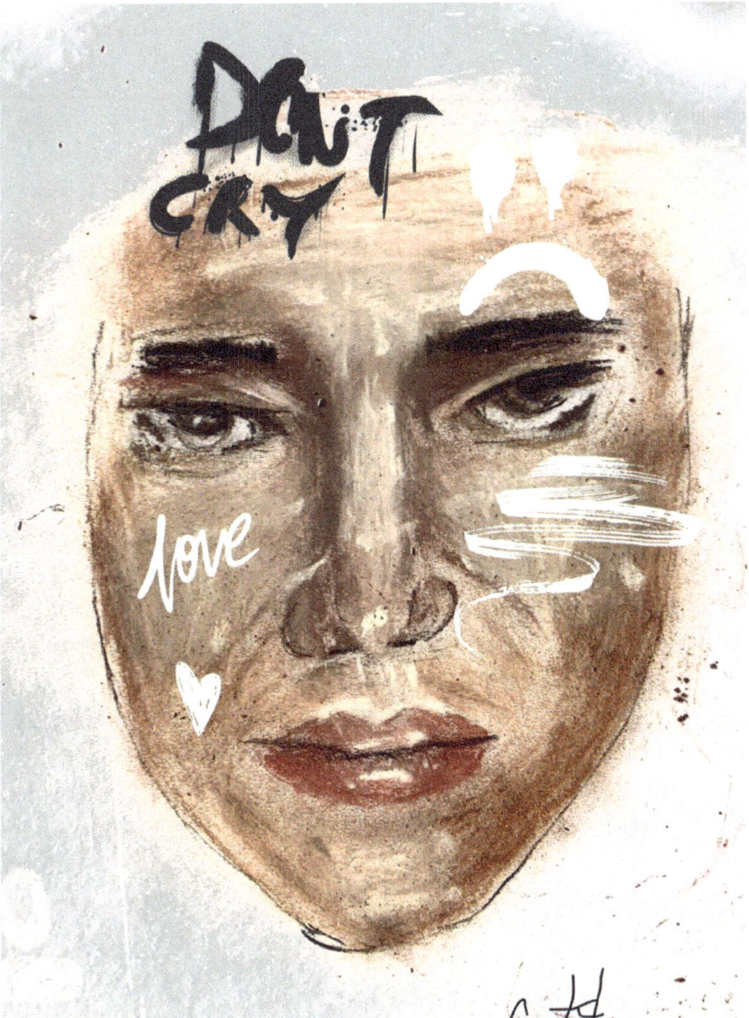
DON'T CRY
love
Cantastina

51

The Path of Discovery

Never ask anyone to be something you can't be yourself.
If you do, you ask them to become someone you cannot.
And you are showing them that your expectations are more significant than your goals.
And once you start asking for things you are not, you will put yourself in a secondary position because your words and ambitions show them that you are not who you asked them to be.

73 Moments in Life

52

Always Remember

Always remember that when you forgive someone, you're not only forgiving yourself, but you are also giving them a chance to change something that they have been inside of them.
The mind works in a funny way.
When we receive forgiveness from a person we hurt, we start to think about and understand our actions.
Those who understand will reflect and change.
Those who need help understanding will show you they believe their decisions were correct.
In the end, by forgiving them, you will set yourself free and see their true colors.
And that is worth more than everything in the world.

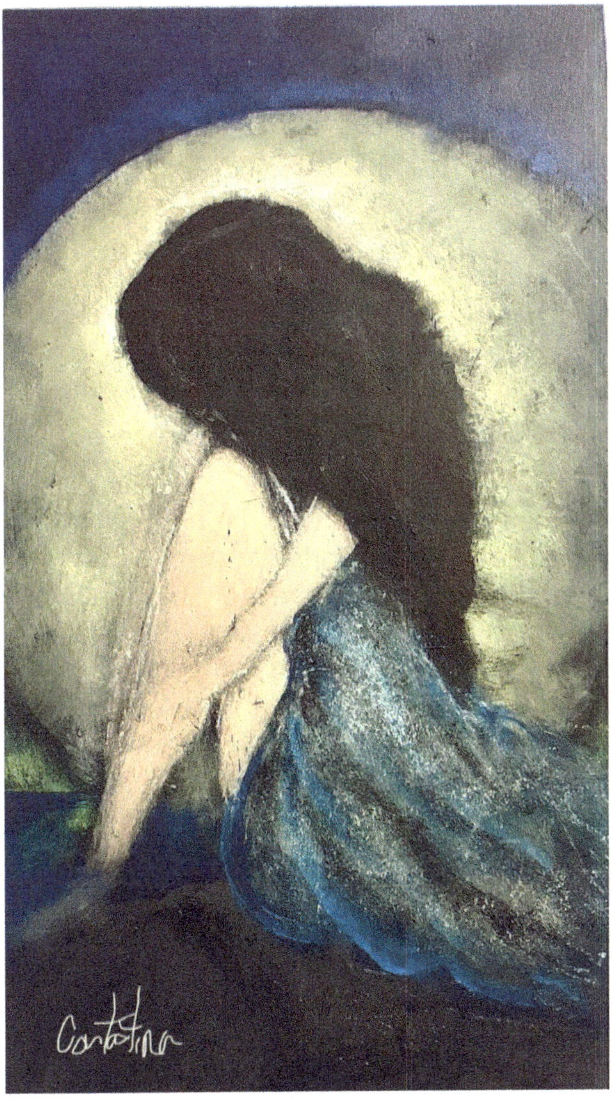

53

Your Perception of Yourself

How you see yourself affects your vibe, thoughts, and reactions to the world.
So, when you love yourself, accept and feel good about your looks, realize that you must build up a real character, not simply having role models, but being you.
It's the most significant step to feel confident, and once you start being confident, you can easily express your talents and show them to the world.
And, whether people like you or hate you, people see the real you, and being able to show the real you is the best vibe ever. People get that.

73 Moments in Life

107

54

People Do This Very Often

People who used to be around you may still be around you now but from a distance.
They still are around, but now you should keep your next steps more private.
They are usually trying to learn about what you are doing.
Sometimes out of curiosity and most of the time from jealousy.
You realize the difference very quickly.
Those who are curious will ask you questions or ask others about you.
Those who are jealous, unable to touch you and what you are becoming, will try to dig up who you used to be because they believe they can stop you from getting to where you're supposed to be.
Learn that they will talk no matter what.
Their lives are uninteresting, so the only way for them to get attention is to look at those who seem more profound and understand the changes that those deeper are experiencing or using the old version of you and trying to keep others away from following your light.

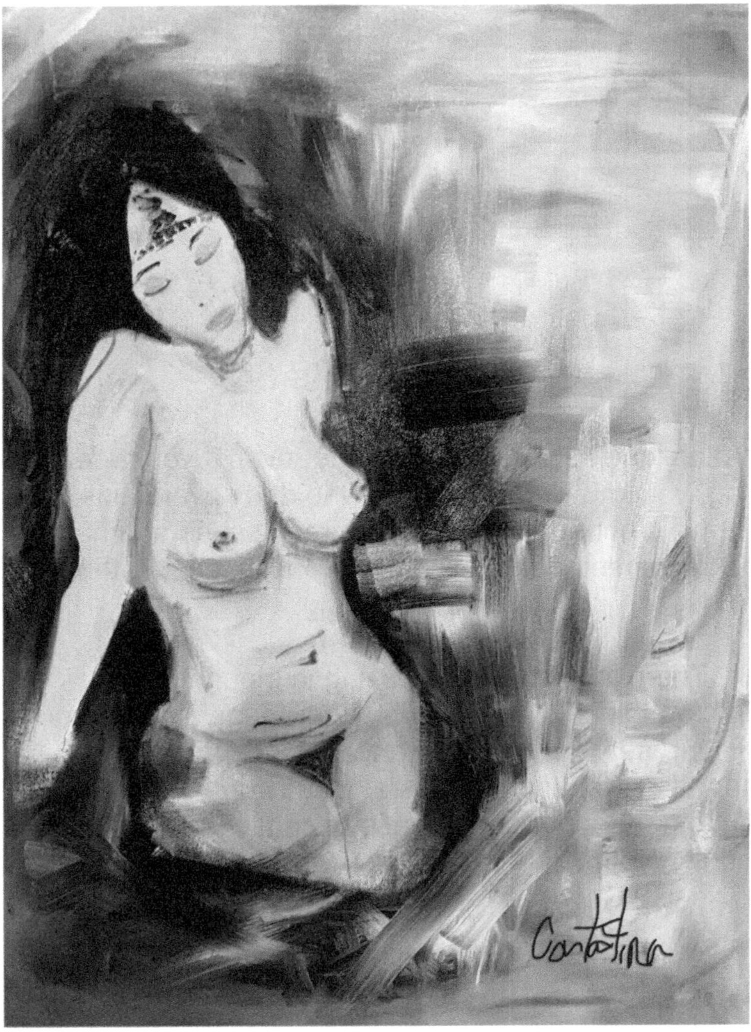

55

Keep Thinking

Learn that as long as you keep thinking, even if you're feeling wrong, you know many people who don't even think.
Many have stopped using their common sense and have turned into sheep eating what the world is feeding them without any filtering.
Don't be like them.
There is a massive blessing in thoughts.
Once you start thinking and seeking knowledge, find it through reading, researching, doing, and looking for solutions.
So, understand that sometimes even a wrong thought can send you to a more important place because it is the starting point of putting yourself in a place you weren't before.

73 Moments in Life

56

The Day You Will Realize

A day will come when you realize that not every action needs a reaction.
Reacting to some things leads you nowhere.
Receiving and holding how people see or think about you usually pushes you to justify yourself when you don't even need to.
Remember, the world is watching.
And most of the time, the world does not need explanations.
Those who need explanations to believe what is right in front of their eyes usually are those who, even if you do, they will still believe the next rumor.
So, stop wasting your energy on things you can't control and start using your energy on things you can handle.
And the things you can control are all inside you.
Nothing you can control is outside you, especially other people's opinions.

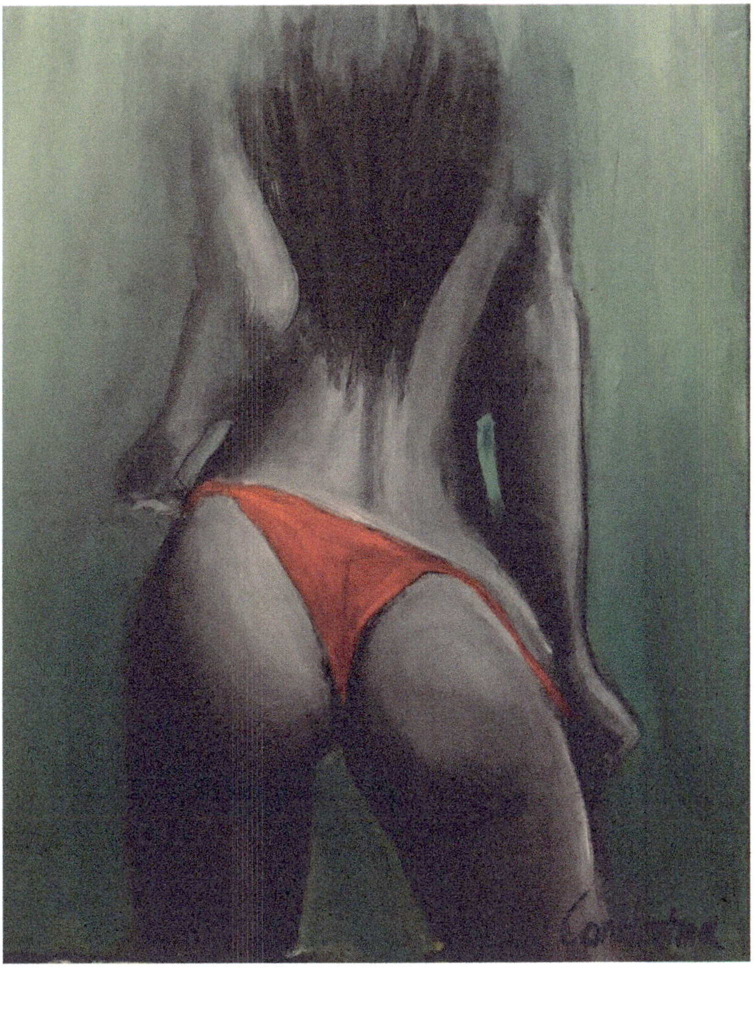

57

Always Remember

Love the way you want to be loved.
Listen to the way you want to be heard.
Give the way you wish to receive.
Care the way you want others to care for you.
And respect like you want to be respected.
Remember that change doesn't start with them but begins within ourselves.

73 Moments in Life

58

Pay Attention to Those

Pay attention to what people say as a joke or out of anger.
This is how they reveal their honest opinions about you.
And what they were dying to say to your face.
Because they didn't have the guts to do it directly, they were waiting for a moment like this to come so they could express themselves.

Dont think
DONT DRESS LIKE THAT
This is right
Just listen
This is wrong
Dont smoke
Dont complain
Your name is
DONT CRY
I AM?
DONT SPEAK
Dont eat too much
CALM DOWN
Eat more, you're too skinny
Dont stay
You're overreacting
DONT ASK WHY
WHY ARE YOU SO COLD?

59

If Your Conversations

When your conversations are about money and business, you will undoubtedly grow in these areas but miss the chance to grow in other vital areas.
Open your thoughts to ideas and motivate yourself to do more. Learn that when you deal with and are healed from the daily things that everyone else is dealing with, your mind is clear to think about goals, ideas, and improvements.
It's essential to grow in those other vital areas.
To have your mind free to grow your dreams and goals, do yourself a favor and don't ignore your personal mental happiness.
Just because you're focused on things that will bring you financial happiness, take advantage of the things that matter.

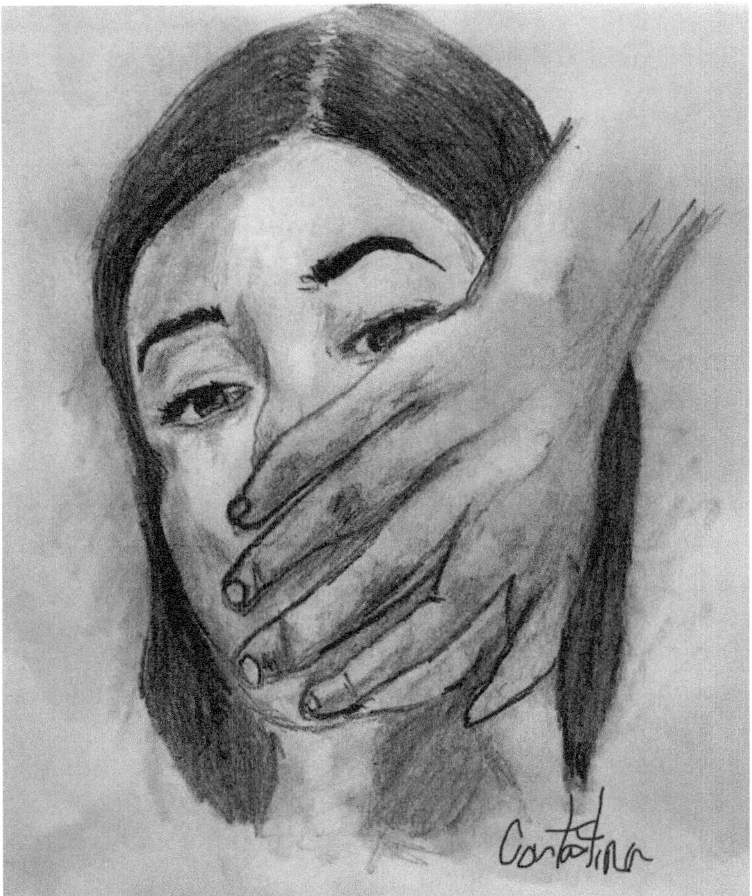

60

A Man Who Truly Cares For You Will Make These Things Happen

First, when he is genuinely sorry, he will change his behavior.
Second, when he misses you, he will make an effort and always show up.
Third, he will never make you feel bad when he loves you.
Fourth, when everyone around him pushes him to stop being with you, he will find a reason to be with you and make it work.
Fifth, he will leave everyone behind to create something great with you.
Sixth, he will walk through fire to be with you.
Learn that what defines a man is not his words but his actions.
Those who are men will find the reason.
The rest will use some cheap excuses, for example, family, culture, respect for his parents, etc.
The reality is that when a man truly cares about you, he cares about being with you.
So, learn that those who use excuses don't care for you.

73 Moments in Life

61

Read This

Everyone loves you when you leave yourself behind.
Also, everyone loves you when you're easy to deal with and not challenging.
But as soon as you set boundaries, apply your requirements, and check if people's words and actions are consistent, everyone starts hating you.
Why?
Because when they recognize that they can't use you, they only have the power to persuade others to stop seeing your value.
So, they start hating, talking, and trying to spread misinformation about you.

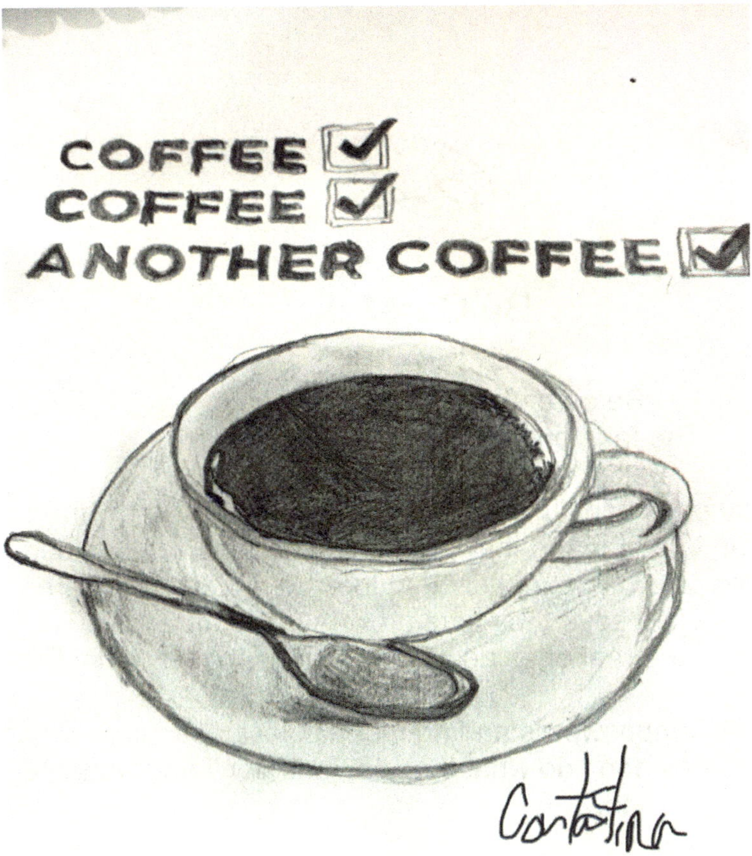
COFFEE
COFFEE
ANOTHER COFFEE

Be Careful

Be careful who you push away.
The fake ones always return with more.
Fake promises and bad intentions.
The real ones usually don't return because they know their value and understand that you don't recognize their value.
They realize that no matter what they do, you will not care.
So, they will save their time proving their value to you.
Remember, the real ones do what they say and say what they do.
No empty words and no meaningless actions.
The fake ones don't do what they say and don't say what they do.

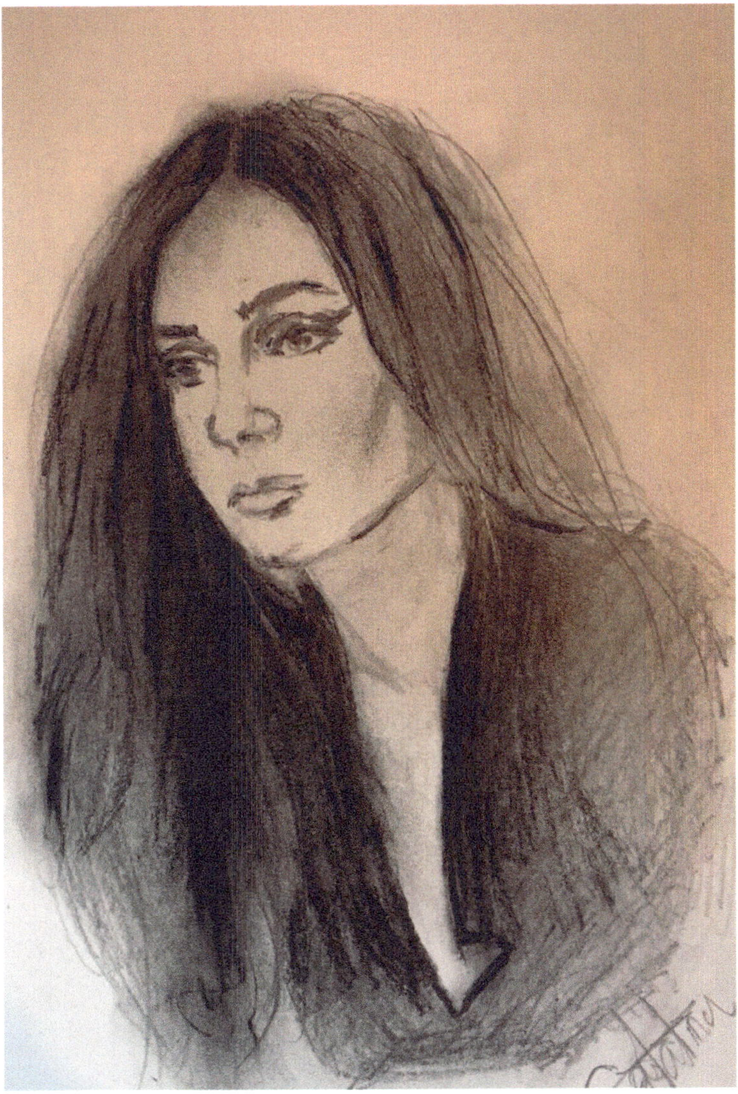

63

If You Ever Meet This Person

If you ever meet someone who trusts no one, remember they once trusted someone with all their heart and were betrayed.
Be kind, patient, and understanding with this person.
It will take time for them to see and realize that you are different from others.
But, once they realize, they will love you forever.

QUEEN
hope
fighter
Queen
Worthy
brave
innocent
hurt
bruised
raped
battered
Self love
afraid
trauma
hitting
Pain
fear
help
trauma
home
partner
kicking
Victim
PTSD
suffering
guilt
children
Victim
stop

64

The Gift of Unspoken Connection

Never tell anyone what you would love to happen.
Never tell them because most of the time, some people try to do these things immediately.
The scary part is that you force some people to manipulate you.
You will see some people start doing things that you would love to happen.
Kisses on the forehead, flowers, and romantic dinners, but you are not seeing who they are and what they want to do.
They do these things not to surprise you but because it comforts them.
Remember that a person's discipline is a part of their character and is expressed in their actions.
They do not need a plan because this is who they truly are.

73 Moments in Life

65

Change as a Catalyst

Learn that change will come.
Learn that change happens every day.
Change can make your life better or worse.
It is up to you whether how you change will make your life better or worse.
If you make the same mistakes, such changes may worsen your life.
If you learn and stop repeating mistakes, such changes improve your life.
Change may be beautiful, but if you keep going down the same road, then change will eat you alive.
Allow yourself to learn, feel free again, and be ready to love.
Just because you had a wrong chapter doesn't mean you have a terrible life.
You are worth more.

73 Moments in Life

66

The Sanctity of Femininity

Never make a woman feel embarrassed for the things she has done with you.
Never make her regret the time, feelings, affection, or appreciation given in your presence.
Otherwise, you will turn a healthy human into something different.
That is, someone will turn into something else and, in most cases, can't return to who they were.
Never forget that each person is responsible for the behavior of many other people in our society.
Love them, appreciate them, and support them throughout your life, just like you love, value, and support your mother.
This may sound hard, but it is very accurate.
Your mother was also a woman for some man.
Think before you step into someone's life.

73 Moments in Life

67

Life Realization

When you create something in life, whether cooperation, investment, friendship, relationship, or anything else, all things need a common beginning.
All things begin with a solid foundation.
A solid foundation is built with trust, effort from everyone involved, consistency, and strong materials or character.
For a foundation to hold during hard times, which will come sooner or later, it must be solid.
So, if you are ready to build something solid, learn that all these are necessary.
If you still decide to build something solid, express it from the beginning.
If others contribute to a solid foundation and you don't, you will create distrust, and the foundation will fail.
Things may go well for a while, but remember that karma is right around the corner.
You're always going to receive back what you give.

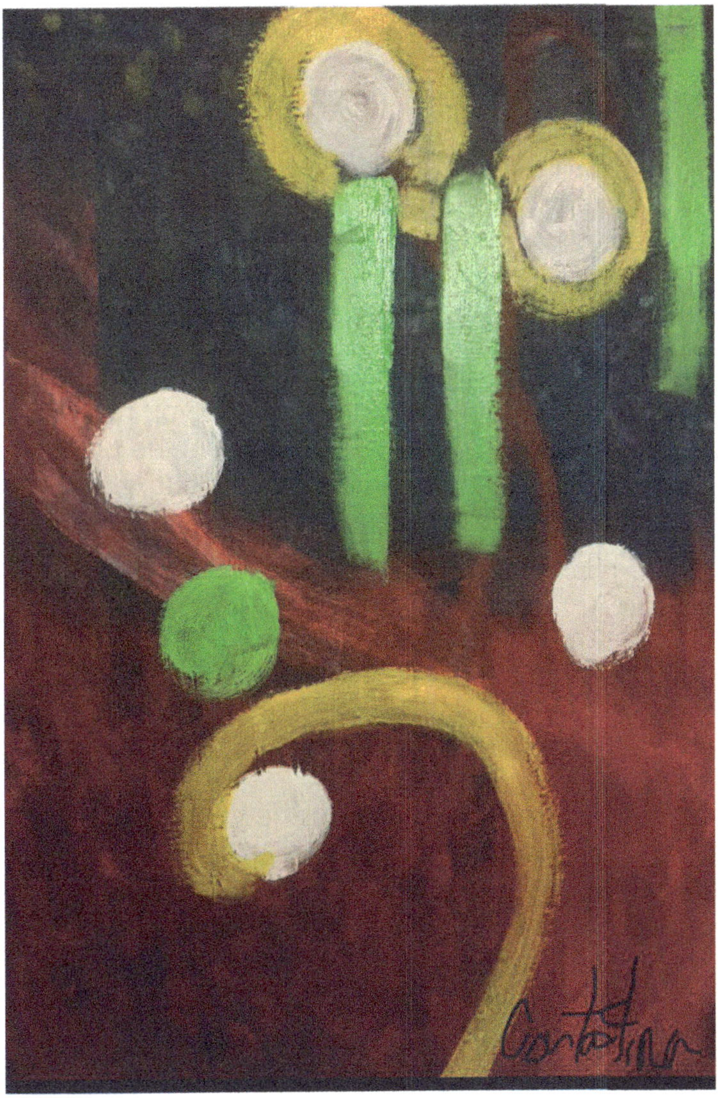

68

Necessary Supplement to Live a Happy Life

No matter your past and no matter what fears you have of tomorrow, always remind yourself that you live in the present. What has happened cannot be changed by thinking, and what may come can only be changed by acting.
Also, what is to come, will come, no matter what, if it is meant for you.
As long as you live in the present, you're helping yourself.
Think straight, act fast, and be aware of the changes right before you.
If you look at yesterday or tomorrow, you may miss everything right before you.
This will create depression, regret, anxiety, and dreams without purpose.
Focus on the things you're creating today, and check on what you have archived today.
Tomorrow is another day.
Today is all that matters.

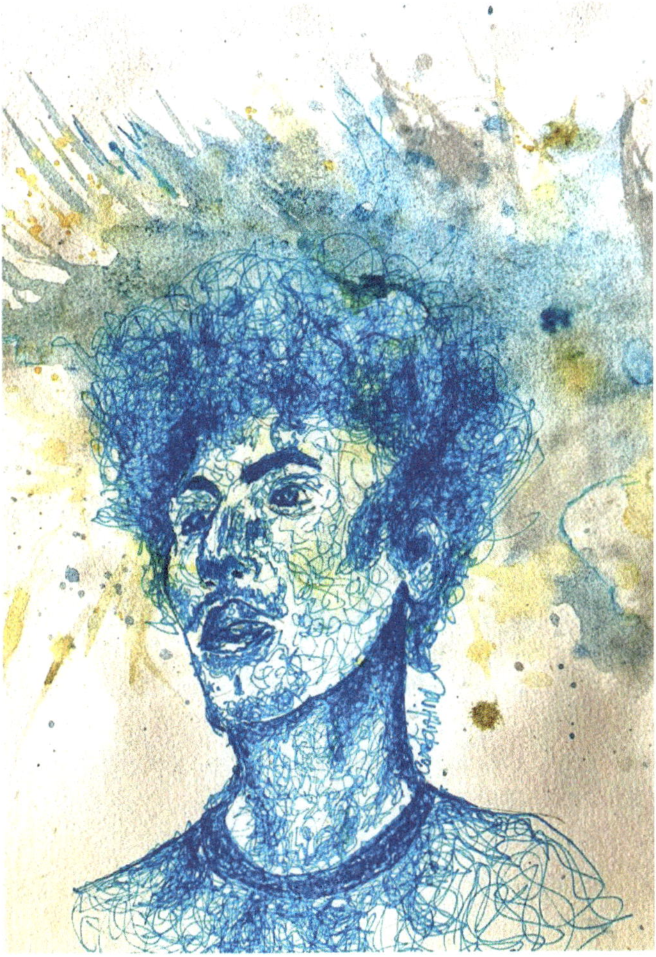

69

The Worse Version of a Person

The worst type of person is someone you will do everything for, but they put you after those who have done nothing for them.
Someone who you will look after, take care of, support, and give all your effort, attention, and appreciation to as no one else has ever done.
Unfortunately, such people have never learned to appreciate people like you.
Learn that you might still be a diamond in the wrong hands but be treated like a stone.

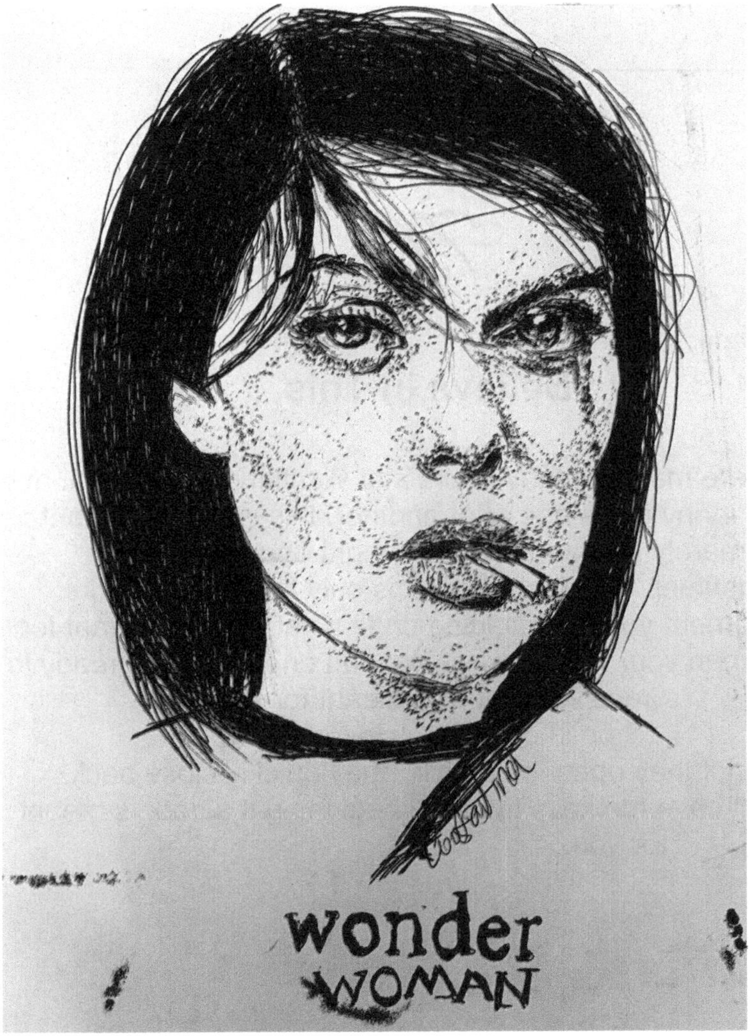
wonder
WOMAN

70

Believe in This

While there may be many doors that you think are for you, and while many close one after another, this is not failure but merely preparation for the right doors to open.
Sometimes you might think it is only for you if it works.
The moment you stop holding on to what was not meant for you is when your thoughts, vision, and energy will be ready to receive what was meant for you.
Stop knocking on closed doors.
Even if they open for a while, they quickly close back.
You will have the keys from the beginning if a door is meant for you.

73 Moments in Life

71

Knowing Who You Are

Knowing who you are makes it even more difficult for people to approach you.
Most of the time, people do not come forward with their true intentions but with fake promises.
So, once they realize that those fake intentions don't work with you, they turn and call you difficult or claim that you don't know what you want from life.
You know what you want from life, but they may not know and love you as you are prepared to know and love them.
So, learn to appreciate yourself. Those who really love and know you will come and stay, and those who don't love and know you will come and go.
And some of those who go may keep hating you from a distance.

73 Moments in Life

72

The Best Advice I Can Give You

Don't be so accessible to so many people.
People don't need to know what you're thinking or doing.
Remember, the more they know, the more you will have to deal with it.
Keep your thoughts, your plans, and your next move private.
Remember that even a single bad vibe from a person can ruin everything.
Always remind yourself that no one can help you deal with it if you can't deal with it.
The hard truth is that most people want to see you down and out.
It is hard to recognize such people; when you do, it is often too late.

73 Moments in Life

73

Stop Checking on Them

Stop checking on them, including what they do, what they post online, and when they are online.
You're creating scenarios in your head that don't exist.
And even if those scenarios exist, you can't do anything about them.
Remember, what anyone does is their own decision.
If they decide to disrespect you, they will disrespect you, whether you check on them or not.
Arm yourself with the power to turn away and leave.
So, if they disrespect you, you are ready to turn away and leave and never look back.
But no matter what, stop checking on them.

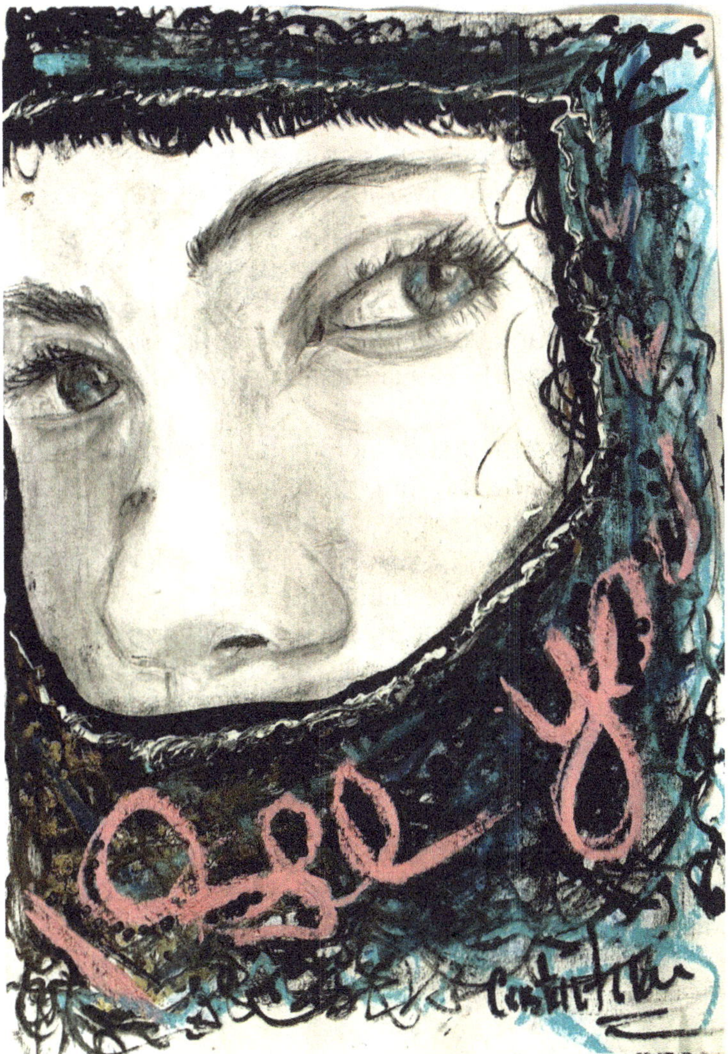

About Asterios Balatzis (Author) (https://asteriosbalatzis.com)

Asterios was born and raised in a small town in Greece.
From a young age, he was always eager to help others, even if they were complete strangers.
Somewhere along his journey, he lost his way and made many mistakes.
He forgot the kindness his mother had taught him, and he became very selfish.
This lasted for many years until he woke up and said, "I don't want to live like this anymore."

So, he changed everything, including his friends, habits, and how he thought about everything.
While the change was not immediate but a journey of its own, it involved losing everything he considered essential and rebuilding himself.
He never backed down from such a challenge. Even when things became tough, and he was continuously tested or possibly dragged back to who he was, he decided to stay on the path and learn many lessons. He focused on creating a new life versus returning to his old life.

The decision to write this book resulted from his influence on many people through his TikTok videos.
So, he started writing with the hope that more people would heal through his influence and the world would have more kind people.

Where do all his thoughts come from? His daily life involves many people, and his work involves interactions with many strangers.
So, he decided to share his thoughts because he has lived unhealed and healed.

About Constantina Constantinou (Illustrator) (https://artbytinaa.myshopify.com/collections/all)

Welcome to the world of Constantina Constantinou, an emerging artist born in Limassol, Cyprus. At 7, she moved to Melbourne, Australia, with her family, where she spent her childhood and received her education. Constantina's passion for art began in school when she discovered the joy of expressing herself through different textures.

Constantina draws her inspiration from women and music, particularly the soulful sounds of blues and jazz. Her artwork celebrates free and expressive women in their unique ways, which she can relate to. Her love for painting women is evident in the majority of her work.

As a dedicated artist, Constantina is always eager to learn new techniques and explore new styles. She has recently delved into abstract art, which she finds particularly enjoyable.

Constantina's art is a reflection of her journey and experiences. Each painting tells a story and captures the subject's essence, whether a woman, a musical genre, or an abstract concept. Explore her work and discover the beauty of her unique artistic style.

Made in the USA
Las Vegas, NV
20 May 2023